MW01629165

WATER, RAILS & OIL

Historic Mid & South Jefferson County

by Dr. Archie P. McDonald

Published for the Port Arthur Historical Society

Historical Publishing Network
A division of Lammert Incorporated
San Antonio, Texas

First Edition

Copyright © 2008 Historical Publishing Network

All rights reserved. No part of this book may be reproduced in any form or by any means, electronic or mechanical, including photocopying, without permission in writing from the publisher. All inquiries should be addressed to Historical Publishing Network, 11555 Galm Road, Suite 100, San Antonio, Texas, 78254. Phone (800) 749-9790.

ISBN: 9781893619609

Library of Congress Card Catalog Number: 2008938660

Water, Rails & Oil: Historic Mid & South Jefferson County

author:	Dr. Archie P. McDonald
cover artist:	Travis Keese
contributing writers for "Sharing the Heritage":	Eric Dabney
	Marie Beth Jones

Historical Publishing Network

president:	Ron Lammert
project managers:	Pat Steele
	Larry Sunderland
administration:	Donna M. Mata
	Melissa Quinn
	Evelyn Hart
book sales:	Dee Steidle
production:	Colin Hart
	Craig Mitchell
	Charles A. Newton, III

PRINTED IN THAILAND

CONTENTS

❖

Kansas City Southern passenger train at the depot at the foot of Procter Street, Port Arthur, in the 1950s.
COURTESY OF THE MUSEUM OF THE GULF COAST, PORT ARTHUR, TEXAS.

INTRODUCTION

❖

A parade celebrating Armistice Day in 1920. The Thornton Hotel (four-story building) was located at 335 Waco on the corner of Procter. O. J. Thornton was the proprietor and manager. The hotel was operated on the European plan, under which the rate included only the room and no food.
COURTESY OF THE MUSEUM OF THE GULF COAST, PORT ARTHUR, TEXAS.

Southern Jefferson County, especially Port Arthur and the Nederland-Port Neches-Groves-Sabine Pass areas, are prime examples of the Gulf Coast culture and economy. Growing up in Beaumont, I have interacted with this area and its citizens all my life. We traveled to its beaches for recreation and friends, relatives worked in refineries and other petrochemical industries located there, and my closest classmates at "Lamar Tech," as we knew Lamar University in the 1950s, called the area home.

Learning more about this exciting area has been a privilege, for which I am indebted to Dr. Sam Monroe, president of Lamar State College-Port Arthur; Lauren Ham, curator and archivist of the Museum of the Gulf Coast; Yvonne Sutherlin, legal and historical researcher; and Ron Lammert, publisher. I thank each for their assistance and confidence.

I appreciate the wealth of information on the area maintained and shared by the Museum, and tours, copying, interpreting, and correcting provided by Lauren Ham and Yvonne Sutherlin. These are the real keepers of the history of an area where Arthur Stilwell, John W. Gates—and countless others—came to live and die by "Water, Rails, and Oil."

Archie P. McDonald

CHAPTER I

IN THE BEGINNING

Before governments, commerce, industry, education, culture, and long before people came to farm and to drill and to refine, land, lakes, rivers, bayous, and marshes circled the Gulf of Mexico. A part of that place, later labeled Jefferson County by a nascent Republic of Texas, remained a natural environment until Native Americans and Europeans arrived to name it and claim it, to parcel it and to develop it.

It is believed that the Paleo-Indians were the first to occupy south Jefferson County approximately 10,000 years ago. What is known about their existence is drawn from the artifacts and fossilized faunal matter that has been collected in this area. Among these, the discovery of Mammoth tusk and Clovis points along the beaches and river beds indicates a culture of nomadic hunters.

Long after the Paleo-Indians, came the Attacapa. They hunted and harvested the bounty of the land and the sea. They built shelters beside fresh water and roamed beaches and savannahs, searching for anything useful for survival. A natural world of birds, reptiles, fishes, mammals, and plants provided sustenance and shelter.

The lives of the Attacapa, or simply "the people" to themselves, cycled for centuries with each generation unaware of how or why their predecessors came to live there, or why others—a few Spaniards and Frenchmen at first, and then great hordes of Anglo-Americans and Asians—arrived to displace them.

The first Attacapa, the Akokisas, and the Deadoses, filtered into coastal territory on both sides of the Sabine River and the Neches River at about the same time as Christ lived beside the Galilee. "Atakapa" means "eaters of men" in Native American language, but likely their cannibalism

CLOVIS CULTURE

The discovery of Clovis Points, or projectiles fashioned by early humans of bone or stone provide evidence of the earliest human activity in South Jefferson County. Clovis Points are so named for the type of projectiles found in association with extinct animal remains in the vicinity of Clovis, New Mexico.

The discovery of artifacts of this prehistoric, Paleo-Indian culture on McFaddin Beach, suggest human occupation of this portion of Jefferson County at the same time as artifacts discovered in New Mexico, or circa 10,000-12,000 B.P. Similar artifacts have been discovered in many other areas of the southeastern United States.

The greatest number of Clovis Points discovered in Jefferson County have been uncovered by wave and storm action on McFaddin Beach. In fact, McFaddin Beach has the highest concentration of Clovis Points in Texas. Dr. Russell Long, a member of the department of Biology at Lamar University, took the lead in discovery and research of these artifacts in the 1970s. This also led to evidence of preserved faunal matter of several extinct species-ranging from mastodon to capybara—suggesting both rain forest and prairie environments in the area during prehistoric eras.

Long Reported, in a monograph published by Lamar University's Spindletop Museum in 1977, the discovery of 166 artifacts—mostly of stone— in the area between Sabine Pass and High Island along the route of U.S. 87. Sixty points have been documented and are on file at the Museum of the Gulf Coast, the Texas Archeological Research Laboratory in Austin, Southern Methodist University, and the Smithsonian Institution.

A Clovis point found on McFaddin Beach by Paul Tanner. Clovis points have been identified with a Paleo-Indian culture dating between 10,000 and 12,000 years ago, long before the Attacapa. The points were used by Paleo-Indians as dart or spear points and were made out of a hard stone, such as flint.

was more ritual than regular diet. They hunted, fished, gathered their victuals, and harvested alligator for its meat, oil, and hide. Early European visitors described the Attacapa as short, dark, and stout, clothed only in breechcloths or buffalo fur, and paired into family units for the rearing of their young.

Attacapa likely numbered fewer than 4,000 in the entire area, at their peak, before European diseases and settlement dropped the population or drove them from the area. Evidence of their time and way of life survives in pottery chards, tools, seashells, and other cultural flotsam gathered by modern archeologists, for none of "the people" remain.

THE COMING OF THE EUROPEANS

Economic, political, and religious stirring in Europe in the fifteenth century quickened that continent's peoples from a near-thousand year sameness in which everyone lived under noblemen who inherited their domain, worshiped through the same church, and earned their bread servicing a feudal system. Nationalism, a religious Reformation, and capitalism brought the quickening, and with it, the first significant efforts of Europeans to venture westward beyond the horizon. Crusades and trade had taken them across the Mediterranean Sea, but the unknown world waiting over the rainbow of the ocean remained a mystery until Christopher Columbus made landfall on islands near the middle of the Western Hemisphere and claimed the land and the sea for Spain. Within three decades Spain had established a New World headquarters in Cuba, Cortez had conquered the Aztecs in Mexico and Pizarro and Almagra the Incas in northeastern South America, and Balboa had crossed the Isthmus of Panama and claimed the vast Pacific for Spain as well.

Spaniards explored the "golden circle" of the Gulf of Mexico, always searching for riches in gold and silver utilized by the superior Native American cultures of the Aztecs and Incas. Alonzo Álvarez de Pineda sailed along the northern coast in 1519, and fashioned the first map of the area. More significantly, survivors of an effort to explore Florida, attempting to reach settlements in Mexico by sailing along the coast, found themselves on

the beach in Malhado, likely Galveston. Only four of them still lived after a few years in the Texas wildness, and one of them, Álvar Núñez Cabeza de Vaca, eventually reconnected with Spaniards and told them stories of golden cities—unseen by Cabeza De Vaca but discussed among the various tribes with whom he had passed nearly seven years as captive and guest. Cabeza De Vaca's stories launched *entratas*, such as the one led by Francisco de Coronado in 1540, still seeking gold but finding instead land ready for grazing. In the absence of immediate available wealth, and in the absence of interest in the area by other Europeans, Spaniards were content to leave Texas alone, as long as that wildness insulated them from English—and especially French—activity elsewhere on the continent.

Then, Frenchmen began arriving on the upper Gulf Coast in the 1680s. LaSalle brought the first of them in 1682 to an area east of the Sabine and the Neches rivers, near the Mississippi River, which they named the Colbert; and then, in 1685, westward, above Matagorda Bay. The French presence, mostly represented by men who traded manufactured goods for fur harvested by Indians, plus a few bonafide settlers, renewed Spain's interest in Texas. They established religious missions and military presidios as signposts to France that Spain owned Texas. The missions struggled for a century, baptized a few Indians, and burned out the zeal of missionaries and presidio soldiers alike. Almost unnoticed, individual settlers such as Antonio Gil Y'Barbo established farms and ranches, usually not far from the missions, and gradually reestablished European economic and cultural ways as adjusted by the new environment. Most of this activity occurred north and west of the lower Neches country. This area was destined to become, early in the twentieth century, the focus of the nation because of oil, an organic source of stored energy and migrated in sands that collected in pools beneath the surface.

ANGLOS ARRIVE

The earliest Anglo-Americans reached eastern Texas late in the eighteenth century after Spain and England had divided French territory in North America at the Mississippi River. Some did so spectacularly, such as filibusters Philip Nolan, who came in the 1790s ostensibly rounding up mustangs for sale in Louisiana, but up to no good, thought Spanish officials, already wary of "Yankee" plots to take Texas from them; or August Magee and his partner Bernardo Gutierrez de Lara, who wanted to establish an independent empire in 1812 at the expense of Spain; or James Long, with the same motive, in 1819. Nolan, Magee, and Long paid the price of failure with their lives.

These spectacular adventures made headlines in eastern American newspapers, but the filibusters who most loosened Spain's grip on Texas came individually and unheralded to

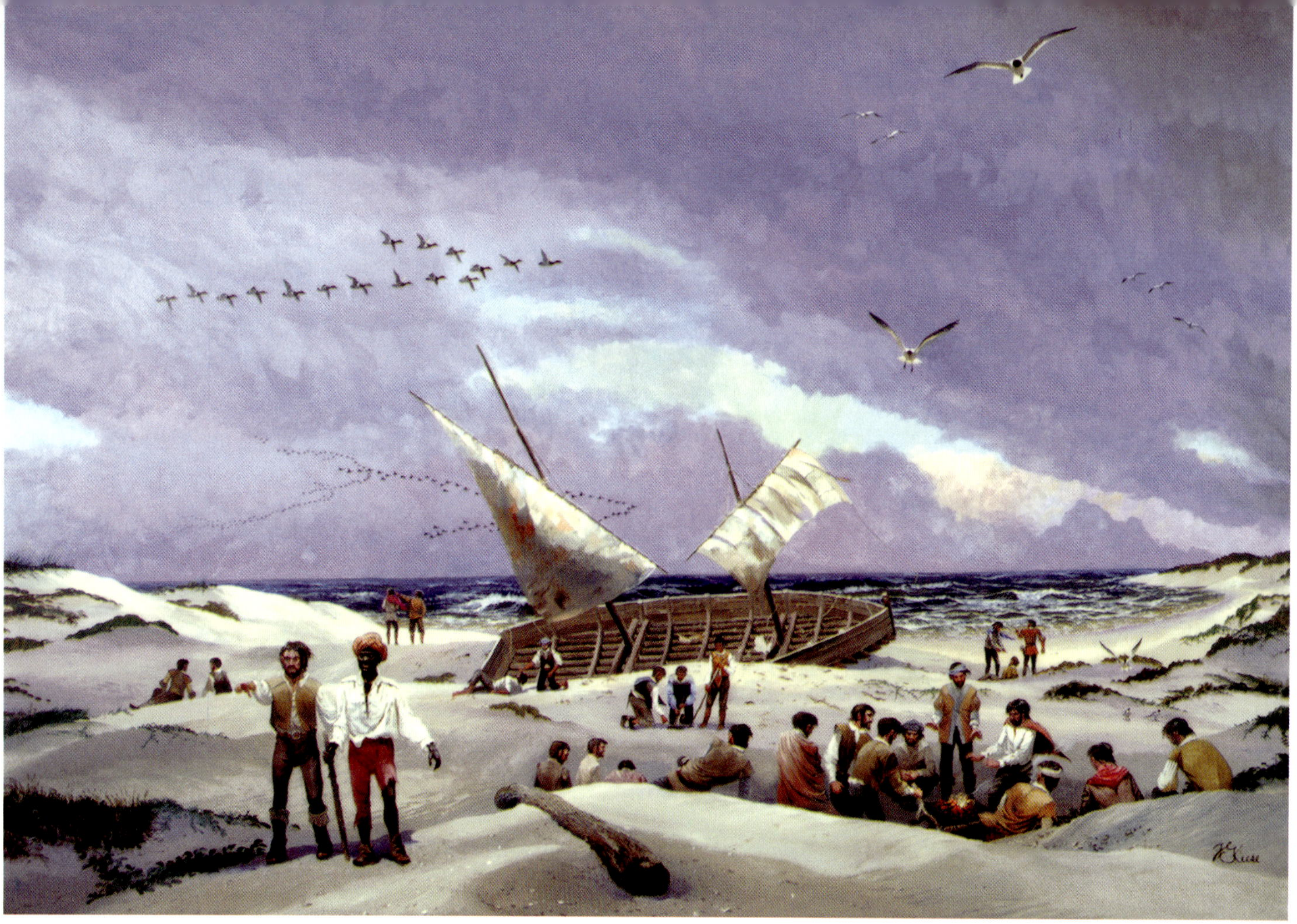

❖

A rendering of Cabeza de Vaca's shipwreck from a mural at the Museum of the Gulf Coast.

PAINTING BY TRAVIS KEESE. COURTESY OF THE MUSEUM OF THE GULF COAST, PORT ARTHUR, TEXAS.

establish homes and farms and ranches. They cared only that the land was available, not which nation claimed it. After Mexico succeeded in shedding Spain's collar in 1821, the arrival of these individual Americans was institutionalized in an empresarial system that permitted, for the first time, legal immigration into a Hispanized Texas. Stephen F. Austin pioneered the system in the lower Colorado and Brazos River Valley, but Haden Edwards secured the first empresarial grant that headquartered in Nacogdoches and extended to the lower Neches valley, and when the Mexican government took the land back in 1827, Joseph Vehlein and Lorenzo de Zavala became empresarios.

Before the decade ended, Thomas Courts received a land grant covering the southern portion of lands destined to become Jefferson County, including the site of the future city of Port Arthur. Already a settlement on Tevis bluff was on its way to becoming Beaumont; John Grigsby had established Grigsby's Bluff, the beginnings of a community later known as Port Neches; and settlements on Cow Bayou, later known as Old Jefferson, had begun by 1835. The Mexican Department of Nacogdoches and the Municipality of Liberty were early seats of government for settlers in the area, though both were located some distance away.

ANGLO DEVELOPMENT

By the mid-1830s, the Indians had mostly perished or left the lower Neches area, Spain and France no longer competed for control, and the more recent American settlers were already anxious for a change in allegiance. Eugene Barker argued that an inevitable cultural clash between Anglo settlers and the Hispanic government produced the Texas Revolution; a more popular belief is that despotism represented by the government of Antonio Lopez de Santa Anna forced Americans in Texas to fight to preserve their "rights," part of their cultural baggage that they presumed had crossed the Sabine River with them.

Protests over Mexico's cloture of American immigration by the Law of April 6, 1830, which caused the very resistance to Mexican authority it intended to prevent, produced military clashes in 1832 in Anahuac, Velasco, and Nacogdoches, conventions in 1832 and 1833 to request separate statehood, further fighting at Gonzales in October and San Antonio in December 1835, and a declaration of independence and the massacre at the Alamo in March 1836. The Battle of San Jacinto, fought seven weeks later on April 21, resulted in the capture of Santa Anna and the establishment of the Republic of Texas under interim President David G. Burnett.

In one of its first actions, the Republic's Congress created county government. Jefferson County was authorized in 1836 and organized a year later on December 21. The original boundaries of the county included all of present-day Orange County on the east, the southern part of Hardin County on the north, the eastern portion of Chambers County in the west, and the shoreline of the Gulf of Mexico in the south. Old Jefferson hosted the county seat for one year, but Beaumont received that assignment in 1838.

Early settlers harvested timber and milled it in the county's first industrial development. Farmers did not find the soils of Jefferson County suitable for the culture of cotton, so stock raising, and later rice production, became the primary agricultural focus, and manufacturing leather goods and building ships added to the industrial base.

NEW SETTLEMENTS

Clusters of settlers began to gather throughout southern Jefferson County. These communities hosted businesses and professional services that supplied the existing population and attracted more. The community known as Port Neches, originally known as Grigsby's Bluff and located on the Neches River approximately ten miles south of Beaumont, occupied a site originally used by the Attacapa as a village. Thomas F. McKinney had intended to establish a community there in the 1830s that he planned to name Georgia, but instead he transferred the property to Joseph Grigsby in 1837. Grigsby developed the river landing into a port facility for Neches River traffic. A gristmill and sawmill represented antebellum industrial development, a foreshadow of the heavy concentration of oil refineries and chemical plants that came to dominate southern Jefferson County in the twentieth century. Grigsby's Bluff, or Port Neches, hosted a Confederate military installation to guard against Union invasion via the Neches River during the Civil War. Grigsby's Bluff served as Confederate Fort Grigsby after the defenses of Sabine Pass were abandoned.

Other settlers developed a community near the mouth of the Sabine River to take advantage of direct access to the Gulf of Mexico. John Bevil attempted to develop what he called the

Jefferson County ranchers periodically drove vast cattle herds through the marsh and bayous to the Gulf of Mexico to swim in the waters along the shore to "debug" them before they were driven to market. Note that cowboys used trained horses to lead the cattle.

COURTESY OF THE MUSEUM OF THE GULF COAST, PORT ARTHUR, TEXAS.

City of the Pass on the banks of the inlet a little more than two miles from the Gulf to Sabine Lake, a natural reservoir that received the waters of the Sabine and Neches rivers and various bayous. Developers had grand plans for numerous public buildings, churches, businesses, and many private dwellings, but they never materialized.

Near the same time, the Sabine City Company, representing the investments of Sam Houston, Philip A. Sublett, George W. Hockley, John S. Roberts, Albert G. Kellogg, Niles F. Smith, and Sidney Sherman—mostly men who had served under Houston in the Battle of San Jacinto—laid out a new settlement directly on the pass from Lake Sabine to the Gulf in 1836. Because of Sabine City's proximity to the Gulf of Mexico, developers hoped it would eventually rival Galveston and other major ports along the Gulf. By the Civil War, the city, now known as Sabine Pass, had shown significant growth. It was connected with rail service via the Eastern Texas Railroad, and had a newspaper—the *Sabine Pass Times*—and such industries as a sawmill in addition to port activities.

The southern county city which ultimately became an industrial giant had one of the most modest beginnings. Promoter Almanzon Huston dreamed of locating a new settlement where Taylor Bayou entered Lake Sabine. Huston purchased the site from Horatio M. Hanks in October 1837, for a new community named Aurora, but little development resulted from his efforts. Later, John Sparks moved his family from Tennessee to the area for a new start in Texas. They arrived at Pavell's Island, located at the junction of Sabine and Neches rivers, where the Pavell family operated a shingle mill. Sparks worked for the Pavell's making cypress shingles until he decided to establish a ferry across Taylor Bayou to take advantage of increasing traffic between Beaumont and the southernmost part of the county.

Sparks' success in the ferry business enabled him to purchase 160 acres from Allen and Nancy Franklin in 1853. Sparks began construction of a house for his family near the planned but as yet undeveloped Aurora, but a fire soon destroyed it. Sparks tried again in 1855, and this time succeeded. In 1859 Sparks' older brother Solomon and his family joined him in Texas, and as his children grew up and married, they also built homes near his original settlement. The Eastern Texas Railroad, constructed in 1861, passed near Spark's settlement, and they named the area Aurora in honor of Almanzon Houston's original plan. During the Civil War workers removed the steel tracks, and other stresses of

that conflict drew business and population from the area. Significant hurricane damage in 1886 resulted in the complete demise of Aurora and the Sparks' settlement.

Meanwhile, William McFaddin, C.C. Caswell, O. M. Kyle, Valentine Wiess, William Wiess, and Samuel Lee organized the Beaumont Cattle Company with McFaddin as manager. The company acquired over 40,000 acres of Jefferson County near its southern and western boundary along the Gulf of Mexico and established one of Texas' largest cattle raising operations at that time. McFaddin interests continue to raise cattle in this coastal area in the twenty-first century.

THE CIVIL WAR

Jefferson County, Texas, hosted one of the most significant battles of the Civil War fought in the Trans-Mississippi Department, or west of the great river, at Sabine Pass.

Modern Texans who look back at the Republic of Texas nostalgically may not remember just how eager the majority of its citizens were to join the Union of the United States and turn over problems with Mexico, Indians, and poor finances to an existing government. They may be more familiar with the efforts of those Texans and others who had joined them—primarily from the South—after little more than a decade to leave that Union and join a new southern Confederacy. Texans generally favored secession by a three to one margin, but the vote in Jefferson County was even more enthusiastic, 256 in favor and only fifteen opposed.

Because Sabine Pass could control access to Beaumont and other settlements in the area from the Gulf of Mexico, Jefferson County and state officials decided to locate Fort Griffin there. It consisted of an earthwork with six cannons to guard the pass. The Davis Guard, or Company F, First Texas Heavy Artillery Regiment, commanded by Captain Frederick Odlum, garrisoned the installation. They marked the channel with stakes and locked their guns on the distance between the markers.

Early in the war United States President Abraham Lincoln proclaimed a blockade of the Confederate coast from the Potomac River on the Atlantic Ocean to Brownsville on the Gulf of Mexico. Union naval and military operations succeeded also in capturing New Orleans and Galveston by mid-1862, though Confederates reclaimed the latter city in January 1863. Meantime, General Nathaniel Prentiss Banks, commanding in New Orleans, decided to send a force of four thousand troops aboard the *Clifton*, the *Arizona*, the *Sachem*, and the *Granite City* through Sabine Pass and up the river to capture the rail connection eastward from Houston, and thus penetrate the interior of Texas.

The Union flotilla approached Sabine Pass on September 8, 1863. With the Davis Guard alert to the danger, Navy Commander Lieutenant Frederick Crocker had no hope of surprising them, so, at mid-afternoon, his vessels approached the Pass in a direct line. The forty-seven men commanded by Lieutenant Dick Dowling, opened fire when the lead vessel, the *Clifton*, came into range in the marked field of fire. The recoil of one cannon took it off its carriage, but the remaining five weapons fired 107 shots at the Union vessels in a little over thirty minutes. A shot exploded the steam boiler of the *Sachem*, leaving her without power and blocking the channel. The *Arizona* withdrew, but the *Clifton* attempted to steam up the pass until a shot destroyed control of the ship's rudder, and it ran aground and further blocked the channel. This caused the *Granite City* to join the *Arizona* in withdrawing to New Orleans with the remainder of Banks' invading army.

❖

A painting of Dick Dowling wearing the Davis Medal awarded to each of the 47 Davis Guard for their heroics in defeating 1,200 Union invaders on September 8, 1963, in the Battle of Sabine Pass. The medals were authorized by Jefferson Davis, president of the Confederacy. A women's group, the Southern Dramatic Association of Houston, supported the project by raising $1,700 to finance the making of the medals by a jeweler in Houston, Charles Gottchalk. The front of the medals featured "D.G." indicating Davis Guard, and a Maltese Cross.

COURTESY OF THE MUSEUM OF THE GULF COAST, PORT ARTHUR, TEXAS.

The Battle of Sabine Pass lasted only two minutes, but its shots were "heard around the world." Coming only two months after significant Confederate losses at Vicksburg and Gettysburg, President Jefferson Davis, in what early in the twentieth-first century is called "spin," hailed Dowling's and the Davis Guard's success as one of the greatest military victories in history because so few had prevailed over so many. The Union did not make another effort to enter Texas from the Gulf of Mexico until the very end of the war, in South Texas, since squadrons based in New Orleans could enforce the blockade in the entire Gulf. Still, the Battle of Sabine Pass provided Texas Confederates, especially those in East Texas, with a moment of triumph in the most significant military action of the war fought in Texas.

Near the end of the nineteenth century, Jefferson County remained agricultural and overwhelmingly rural, though several port cities, notably Beaumont, Grigsby's Bluff or Port Neches, and Sabine Pass prospered and increased in population because of water and then rail transportation. Cattle raising and wood processing dominated economic activities, and county government was well established. Schools and churches provided education and religious services, the population grew rapidly from immigration from southeastern states and from biology—large families of six or more children were common—all combining to make hope for even greater growth likely to have a positive outcome. Few residents of the county could have imagined that on January 10, 1901, the long proclaimed and often ridiculed predictions of Patillo Higgins that oil awaited in a salt dome located a few miles south of the county seat came true, or what its discovery would mean to southern Jefferson County.

A rendering of the Battle of Sabine Pass from a mural at the Museum of the Gulf Coast.

PAINTING BY TRAVIS KEESE. COURTESY OF THE MUSEUM OF THE GULF COAST, PORT ARTHUR, TEXAS.

CHAPTER II

"Into the Jefferson County scene in 1895 came Arthur Edward Stilwell, erstwhile successful insurance salesman, head of a transportation system and trust company, and believer in dreams, hunches, and the supernatural creatures that he called 'Brownies' to build what he later described as 'the only city ever located and built under directions from the spirit world....'"

This is how writers for the Works Projects Administration introduced Arthur Stilwell, founder and namesake of Port Arthur, Jefferson County's second largest city and industrial and business anchor of the southern portion of the county.

Stilwell came from a family highly placed in the post-Civil War, entrepreneurial era. One grandfather had helped construct the Erie Canal and the New York Central Railroad and helped found Western Union, and his father became a successful businessman in Rochester, New York. Despite his background, Stilwell's success in business—at least until he lost control of the Kansas City, Pittsburg, & Gulf Railroad, and with it his place as patron of Port Arthur—came largely from his own ingenuity and effort; however, he attributed his achievements as much to the "Brownies." Stilwell and others may well have credited supernatural guidance with business success, as others have prayed to a different deity, but likely hard work, experience, and luck enhanced his intuition and made success possible.

Stilwell's formal education ended, by his estimation, at approximately the fourth-grade level due to childhood illness. He often traveled to New York City with his father on business trips, which brought him into his grandfather's world, where he made the acquaintance of such men as George Pullman, manufacturer of railroad rolling stock, who later played a role in Stilwell's achievements in establishing railroad lines.

Stilwell left home at the age of sixteen to work in the billiard room of the Southern Hotel, then returned to New York City to a job with a novelty distributor. Stilwell next purchased a printing business and learned all phases of that business from layout to sales to production. Perhaps his

Port Arthur's Procter Street looking eastward from about the 300 block, April 24, 1897. Joseph Bash's grocery and hardware store is the first two-story building on the right. The young town backed up to Lake Sabine and Bash stated that if he didn't make at least fifty cents before noon he would close the store and pick up either a fishing pole or a gun and walk out and get fish or game for his family's evening meal.

COURTESY OF THE MUSEUM OF THE GULF COAST, PORT ARTHUR, TEXAS.

inspiration came from a Brownie, or just good observation, but Stilwell noticed that advertisements for local businesses appeared on all schedules for New York Central trains, but that most railroads in the South did not carry them. He convinced several railroads in Virginia to allow him to print their schedules without cost to the railroads in return for his selling and keeping the revenue for advertisements, plus a pass on the trains to make his sales rounds.

Printing schedules taught Stilwell, who had a quick mind despite its lack of formal education, a great deal about the operation of railroads. "On a hunch," Stilwell wrote in an autobiography, he decided to move to Kansas City and build a rail connection to the Gulf of Mexico to give midwestern farmers access to the international market for shipping their abundant crops of grain.

Stilwell arrived in Kansas City with $25,000, an inadequate sum to finance his scheme to reach the sea, so he engaged in several other enterprises to accumulate necessary capital. He founded the Kansas City Suburban Belt Line and Grand Central Railway Station, offering public transit to the city's growing population. Next came coal mines located near Hume, Missouri, both for the product and the business of hauling the fuel most in demand in the last quarter of the nineteenth-century.

With sufficient capital to begin his dream, in 1895 Stilwell and his investors considered building their railroad, the Kansas City, Pittsburg & Gulf Railroad (the "PEEGEE" in railroadese), south to Shreveport, then purchasing Paul Bremond's Houston, East & West Texas Railroad, completed from Houston to Shreveport in 1883. The HE&WT ("Hell Either Way Taken") also had a direct connection to the Gulf waters at the Port of Galveston. Stilwell rode the HE&WT to investigate the line and port facilities, and at first found everything satisfactory; he made an arrangement with the Galveston Terminal Company for shipping and took an option on the rail line. Before he presented the business plan to his board of directors in Kansas City, however, Stilwell's Brownies intervened.

Stilwell claimed to have experienced a dream in which he received a message to abandon the proposed arrangement with the HE&WT because Galveston would soon be destroyed by a storm. Instead, Stilwell sensed, he should build his own rail line more directly south from the southwestern route of the existing line, locate his terminal inland on the north shore of Lake Sabine, and dig a canal connecting its port facilities with Sabine Pass, which was located much nearer open water and more vulnerable to tropical storms and hurricanes. The canal should be located on the western shore, said the Brownie, and its excavated earth pushed to the west to help protect shipping from storms on the lake.

Stilwell attempted to purchase land for facilities in Sabine Pass from Herman and Augustus Kountze, developers of the Sabine and Eastern Railroad which served passenger and freight users between Sabine Pass and Beaumont, but they did not reach an agreement. Enroute home to Kansas City on the Kountzes' railroad, when the train passed the north shore of the lake, Stilwell told a traveling companion, "This is the future terminal of our road." He designated locations for wharves and docks and decided that the new city would be known as "Port Arthur."

Hearing Stilwell's report, his board of directors abandoned the purchase of the HE&WT and authorized $2 million for the purchase of land and facilities under the corporate direction of the Port Arthur Townsite and Land Company. The company acquired 4,000 acres through a subsidiary, the Port Arthur Canal and Dock Company, purchasing "all the land between the townsite and Taylor Bayou." The company laid out the townsite on the memories of old Aurora. The new city's first residents lived in tents while they built more permanent shelter. Joseph Bash opened a general store, the city's first, in May 1896, in the 300 block of Procter Street, named in honor of soap manufacturer Colonel William

Procter, whose name remains associated in the twenty-first century with Procter & Gamble, a mega business and international enterprise. At the time, two plowed furrows represented what eventually became Port Arthur's "main street" and center of its retail and professional activity during the first three quarters of the twentieth century. Peter Stock's Port Saloon, located on the corner of Procter and Austin Avenue, joined Bash's store, and E.A. Laughlin opened a lumberyard, all before the month ended. The birth of Arthur Stilwell Smith, the city's first recorded birth, may not have been the result of a Brownie, but it was a good omen nonetheless.

By March 1897, Stilwell had completed the Kansas City, Pittsburg & Gulf's first depot in the city, the first pier, Hotel Sabine, and a large natatorium were under construction and deep-water wells were completed. To help in the development of agriculture in the area, Stilwell hired Frank Hammon, superintendent of the Darby Fruit Company of Kansas City, to establish an experimental farm near Port Arthur. Hammon did so on a three-hundred-acre tract, later known as Griffing, and began experimenting with the growth of vegetables, fruit trees, and tobacco.

Stilwell's Experimental farm located on 320 acres, now Griffing Park. Frank Hammon, of the Darby Fruit Farm in Kansas City, Missouri came to Port Arthur in 1896 and laid out the vegetable and flower gardens and fruit orchards. Due to the excellent soil and climate conditions, potatoes, beans, peas, figs, oranges, lemons, limes, citrons, and pomegranates were grown for the market. John W. Gates later purchased the Farm, renamed it Port Arthur Nurseries, and began selling trees and plants. He gave the city 1,000 eucalyptus trees to be planted along the streets, having grown some 17,000 for market.

COURTESY OF THE MUSEUM OF THE GULF COAST, PORT ARTHUR, TEXAS.

The founding of the *Port Arthur News* on March 18, 1897, and of the *Port Arthur Herald* one day later, the city's first newspapers, and a post office, provided evidence of continued growth, as did the beginning of the city's first regular Christian religious services by the Reverend W. F. Rentz, a Lutheran, who was soon joined by members of the First Methodist Episcopal Church. Also that March, men from the community donated labor and materials and erected the city's first schoolhouse on land provided by the Townsite Company—in a single day! Peter Stock, unable to leave his saloon, sent beer for the refreshment of the workers.

What Port Arthur needed most was people, so the PeeGee ran excursion trains from Kansas City, bringing hundreds of prospective new residents to the area. The *Port Arthur News* beat the rival *Herald* to press by one day, distributing its first issue to passengers on the first excursion train before they reached the city. The editor welcomed them with, "Port Arthur is yours, or at least as much as you are able to pay for…. Take everything you fancy except the townsite…. Keep off the grass. Don't shoot at the mosquitoes. This is the closed season under Texas law."

The next day, the *Herald*'s editor welcomed excursionists even more poetically: "Beautiful Lake Sabine is as changeable as the moon, as fickle as a woman, and gives us every day a new and different aspect of its beauty. At times, beneath a gray and misty sky, it lies with a sullen face like a sulky child. Then comes a burst of sunshine, the clouds vanish and the little breezes dimple its face to smiles…."

PORT ARTHUR AND STILWELL'S CANAL

Arthur Stilwell founded his city by Sabine Lake in 1895, and it grew rapidly. A census taken in 1898 counted over 1,100 residents, enough to justify incorporation of the City of Port Arthur and election of the town's first mayor, Nat R. Strong. Workers completed construction of a roundhouse for the PeeGee and Hotel Sabine.

Fulfilling Stilwell's dream required completion of the canal necessary to make Port Arthur a seaport, but legal objections from the Kountze brothers succeeded in delaying completion of the canal. Stilwell had the permission of the Corps of Engineers to construct the canal, "so long as it does not interfere with the riparian rights of owners of lands adjoining." Kountze interests sued Stilwell and obtained a series of injunctions that

Port Arthur businessmen celebrate the last cut through the marsh for the canal from Sabine Pass to Taylor Bayou, 1899. In the photo are E. A. Laughlin, H. H. Beels, Billy Farrell, L. Schuh, A. H. Scott, Peter Stock, A. J. M. Vuylsteke, M. R. Box, Colonel Jim Furlong, J. W. Carr, Hans Falkenburg, A. Spence, W. A. Hall, Joseph Bash, Julius Holmes, Jack Campbell, Doctor Barraclough, Doctor Hughes, Judge J. B. Bennet, W. L. Carr, Mr. Cleveland, Mr. Chronister, Mr. Haggerty, and Mr. Turner.

COURTESY OF THE MUSEUM OF THE GULF COAST, PORT ARTHUR, TEXAS.

Left: The S.S. Saint Oswald *being loaded at Port Arthur docks August 13, 1899. The* Saint Oswald *was the first steamer to dock in the new port after the canal was completed from Sabine Pass. The captain was W. P. Curtis of South Shields, England. This photograph was taken by Frank Trost who became known world wide for his photo of the Lucas Gusher at Spindletop on January 10, 1901.*
COURTESY OF THE MUSEUM OF THE GULF COAST, PORT ARTHUR, TEXAS.

Below: *Rice farming in Jefferson County. Note the intricate levee system used to control water levels for various growth stages of the rice.*
COURTESY OF THE MUSEUM OF THE GULF COAST, PORT ARTHUR, TEXAS.

delayed and then halted construction of the canal. They claimed that the canal would cause greater silting from the Sabine and Neches rivers, especially at their end of Sabine Pass. So Stilwell abandoned the original plan to dredge on the west side of Lake Sabine and instead moved inland to land already controlled by the Port Arthur Canal and Dock Company.

Work on the canal began at Taylor Bayou with the intention of constructing the canal all the way to Sabine Pass, but another injunction

slowed the work once more. Meantime, Stilwell's dock company, already completed, remained busy despite such legal entanglements. With the PeeGee bringing grain from the Midwest and timber production in the area, workers at the pier on Houston Avenue had plenty to do loading thousands of bales of cotton, tons of flour and corn, and millions of board feet of lumber on barges that tugs pushed to ocean vessels waiting at the southern end of Sabine Pass.

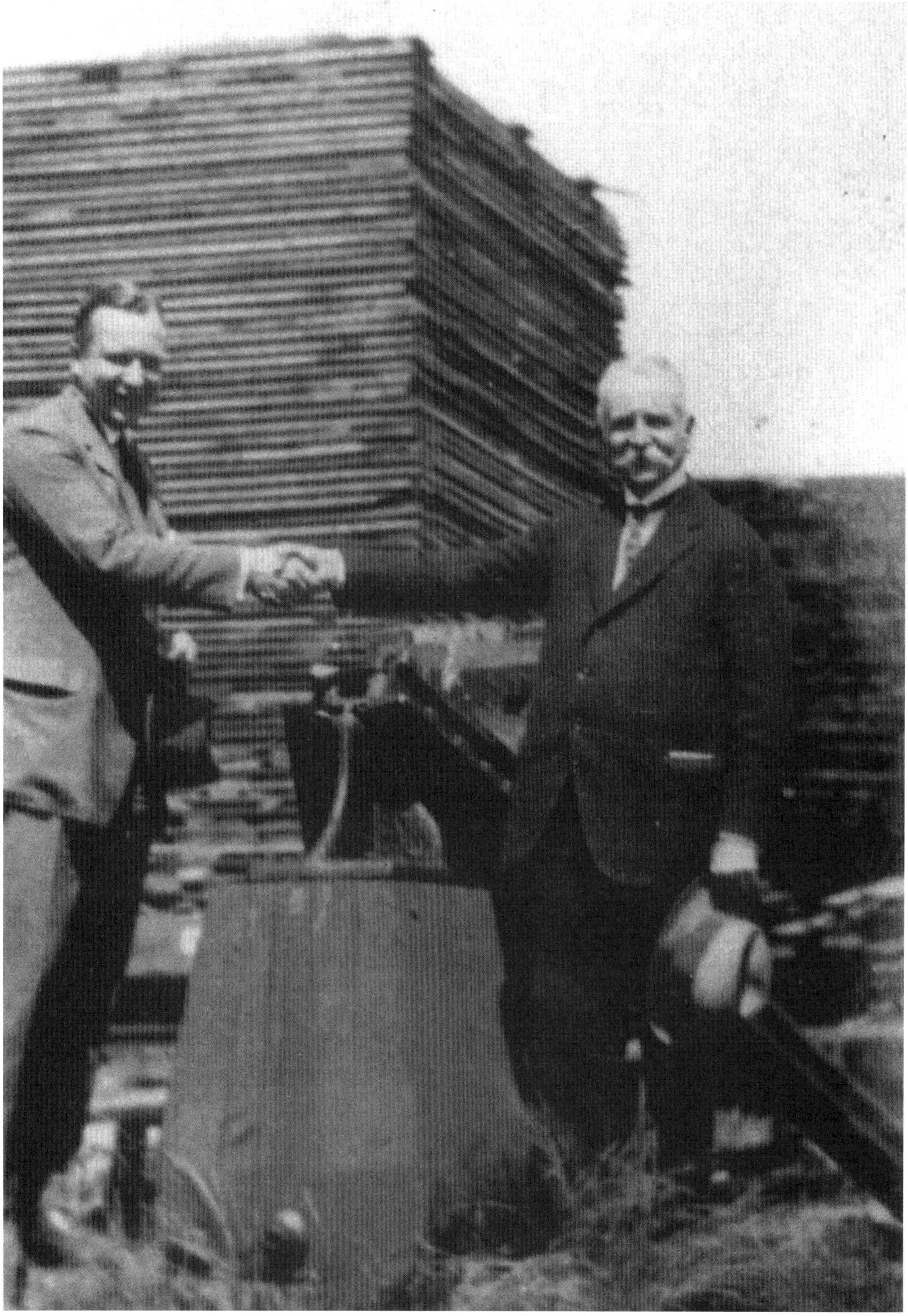

Port Arthur's growth was evident in the completion of the Hobo Line, a local transportation system for workers, beginnings of cultivated oyster beds, a fish oil plant, Horace L. Rodgers theatre, an electricity plant, banks, a telephone service, and grain elevators. Citizens expressed pride in the luxury of Hotel Sabine. The *Herald*'s editor said, "The hotel ranks among the best in the South, and its reputation is well devised...In the main building, which is three stories high, there are thirty sleeping rooms and a large parlor. The annex contains forty sleeping rooms."

With the latest and they hoped the last injunction obtained by the Kountze brothers lifted, work resumed on the canal in January 1899. By February, with the work approximately half completed, the Kountze brothers sought the assistance of Secretary of War Russell G. Alger, who had authority over the Corps of Engineers. The Kountzes claimed this time that silt from Taylor Bayou, not the rivers, would harm their interests. The canal company's engineer, Robert Gillham, claimed that a hundred years would pass before even a foot of silt could collect in the Pass, so while awaiting word from Alger, the dock company went back to work on the canal— from both ends to hasten its completion— anticipated by March 10. The day before, as townsite manager George Craig watched the opposing dredges draw near each other from Hotel Sabine, he learned of the approach of a boat bearing Charles Quinn, engineer in charge of Sabine Pass, to halt the work once more.

Craig waited for Quinn while Gillham raced to the work site to urge haste on the workers, sweetening the plea with an offer of a $100 bonus if they completed the canal on time. Meantime, Craig entertained Quinn at the hotel, and when the engineer finally mentioned the desist order, Craig declined responsibility, suggesting that he deliver the order directly to the dredge operation. The delay proved sufficient for the completion of the canal, which officially opened on March 25, 1899. The first ocean vessel, the British ship *St. Oswald*, steamed up the canal to Port Arthur's grain elevator in August and loaded grain, flour, barrel staves, and planed lumber consigned to Rotterdam.

NEW SETTLEMENT AND CONTINUED DEVELOPMENT

With Port Arthur properly launched and its seaport status secured by the new canal to Sabine Pass, Stilwell turned to additional development to support the operation of the Kansas City, Pittsburg & Gulf Railroad.

❖

A map of Port Arthur, 1897.
COURTESY OF THE CITY OF PORT ARTHUR ENGINEERING DEPARTMENT.

❖

As a tribute to the heritage of Nederland settled by immigrants from Holland in 1898, citizens of the city erected a replica of a Dutch windmill in 1970. The site was dedicated to actor and singer Tex Ritter, who lived in Nederland, in 1977. The windmill houses a museum which pays tribute to the city's beginning and displays artifacts dating back over 100 years.
COURTESY OF THE NEDERLAND
CHAMBER OF COMMERCE

A significant portion of Stilwell's financial support came from investors in the Netherlands, so he decided to build a community near the Gulf of Mexico specifically to receive immigrants from that north European and maritime nation. The Port Arthur Township Company laid out street patterns at a site seven miles south of Beaumont that they named Nederland. George Rienstra arrived from the Netherlands first in November 1897, and before the month ended forty more Netherlanders had joined him. They established truck and dairy farms and eventually many turned to the cultivation of rice, which became the leading non-animal agricultural crop in Jefferson County during the next century.

In addition to such international diversity, the first African Americans took up residence in Port Arthur in July 1898, with Lawrence Alexander, an employee of the city water works, among the first. By the end of that year the city's population had risen to approximately 1,800, and a volunteer fire department with 35 willing firefighters stood ready to assist Chief George Stearns suppress destructive fires. First Bank of Port Arthur, later known as First National Bank, offered financial services from its location on the corner of Procter Street and Austin Avenue; the Port Arthur School Board, with D.G. Parker as president, took over administration of schools in the south county area; and before the year ended, founders Charles Ashley, E. L. Rothrock, W. E. Hall, E. F. Vilkmer, J. W. Carter, and W. M. Smith organized the Board of Trade—later the Greater Port Arthur Chamber of Commerce—and named George M. Craig its first president.

In the last five years of the nineteenth century, south Jefferson County experienced more change and economic development than had occurred during all previous millenniums. Out of the ruins of old Aurora, visionary Arthur Stilwell followed his hunch, his intuition, his Brownies, from the heartland to the sea. He built an inland port and connected it to the world via Sabine Pass. Industry, especially if connected to exporting, retail development, public and private utilities, and other services—including city water, electricity, and telephone, a new communication device—were in place. New towns and increasing population evidenced a bright future for Stilwell's dream. Even Stilwell and his Brownies did not foresee changes just over the horizon in the new century that would be wrought by oil and steel.

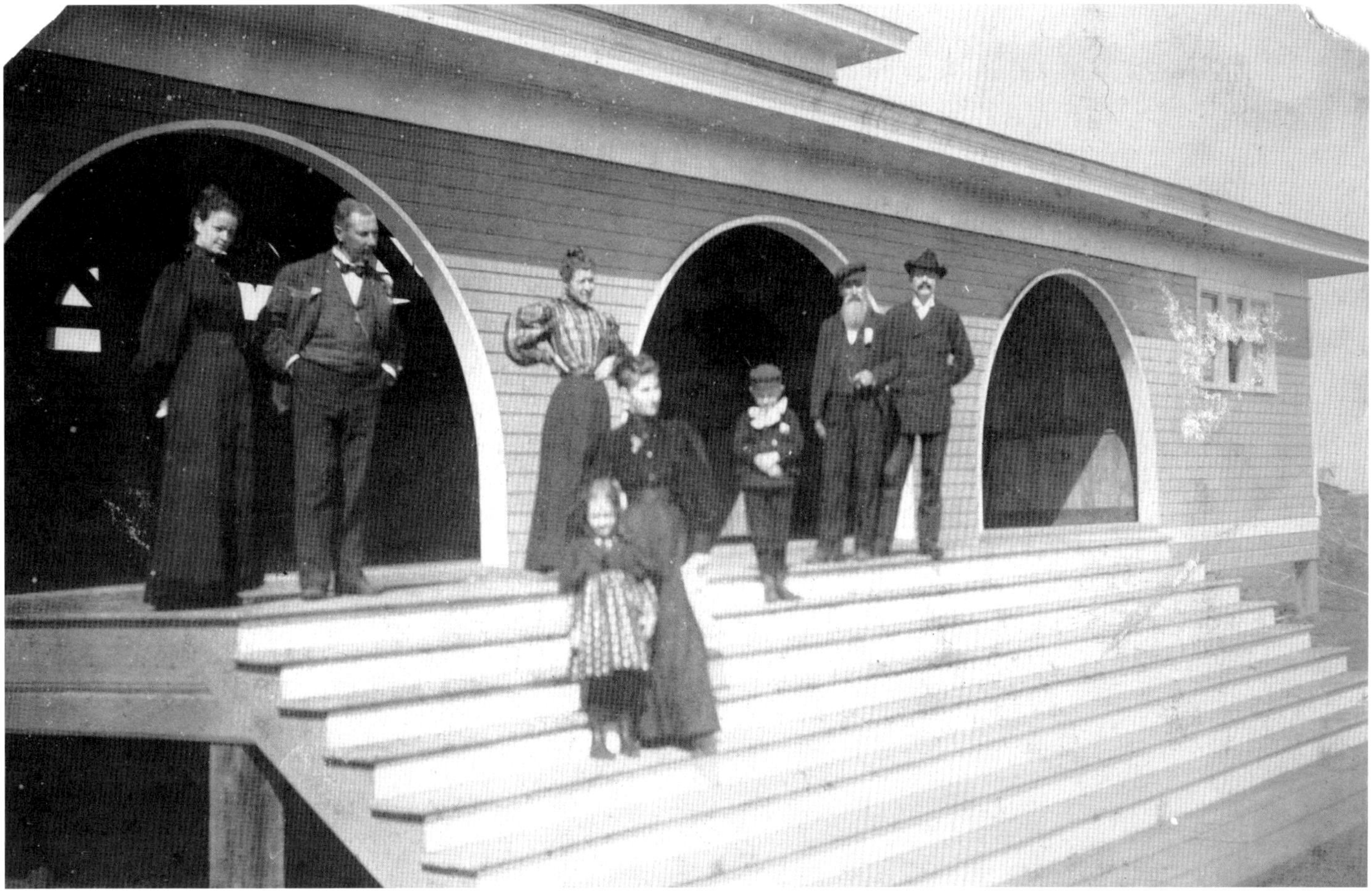

CHAPTER III

STEEL

A powerful new force reached southern Jefferson County in December 1899, one whose role as an urban developer eventually equaled that of Arthur Stilwell. On December 3, John W. Gates arrived in Port Arthur to inspect the city's canal and shipping facilities. Gates told those who attended a banquet at Hotel Sabine on December 3 that what he had learned pleased him, but that more could be accomplished with additional capital—capital Gates knew he could supply. Before his death in 1911, Gates had taken over Stilwell's railroad and urban development interests and eliminated his influence over affairs in the southern portion of Jefferson County.

John Warne Gates grew up on the farm where he was born on May 8, 1855, in DuPage County, Illinois, near the rural community of Turner Junction. In almost a Horatio Alger template, even as a youth Gates demonstrated entrepreneurial skills and salesmanship, qualities that in maturity made him one of America's wealthiest men. Such traits were manifest in Gates' trading various items with other youths, mostly driving a sharper bargain than did his playmates. At the age of eighteen, Gates purchased partial interest in a used threshing machine and also developed a business as a distributor of wood. At twenty he became the proprietor of a hardware store in St. Charles, Illinois, and there met Isaac L. Ellwood, a wholesale hardware dealer of similar interests and energy.

Ellwood had acquired manufacturing and distribution rights to a barbed wire invented by Joseph Glidden. He hired Gates as a salesman, and Gates traveled to Texas in 1876, a year of new beginnings in the "Reconstructed" state. By then the great Texas cattle drives to Abilene and Dodge, Kansas, and

Left: Isaac L. Ellwood, one of the first successful commercial producers of barbed wire and builder of the Pompeiian Villa. Ellwood's wife refused to live in Port Arthur because of the rain and the mosquitoes. He sold the palatial home to James Hopkins, President of the Diamond Match Company, who, in turn, traded the house to George Craig for Texas Company stock.
COURTESY OF THE MUSEUM OF THE GULF COAST, PORT ARTHUR, TEXAS.

Center: John W. "Bet-a-Million" Gates, financier. Gates built the Mary Gates Memorial Hospital on Lakeshore Drive in 1909 in memory of his mother. He also founded Port Arthur College in 1909. Gates realized that the men on the ships transporting oil around the world could not talk to each other. He opened the school to teach wireless telegraphy to the seamen and also to teach young women office skills so they could work in the business world. Gates died suddenly in Paris in 1911.
COURTESY OF THE MUSEUM OF THE GULF COAST, PORT ARTHUR, TEXAS.

Right: Dellora Gates, wife of "Bet-a-Million" Gates. In January 1916 Mrs. Gates announced that she was donating $25,000 to build and maintain a public library in memory of her husband and their son, Charles. Charles died in 1913 in a New York railroad station.
COURTESY OF THE MUSEUM OF THE GULF COAST, PORT ARTHUR, TEXAS.

other railhead towns had been underway a decade, and cattle spreads stretched westward and north to the state's borders with New Mexico and Oklahoma. Most of that territory did not afford sufficient timber or rocks for fencing, standard natural materials readily available in the eastern United States; if they had been available in the West, likely labor intensity would have made them unaffordable. Barbed wire provided a solution, but cattlemen worried that such small strings of steel could not contain their heavy livestock, especially a bull or a cow determined to reach the other side of such a fence. They were correct, of course, but Gates knew that cattle would honor the fence if they could see it, so he engaged cattlemen in San Antonio in an experiment—a bet, really—to demonstrate the effectiveness of his product. He enclosed a few animals in a small, fenced area in a public square. When the scheme worked, Gates achieved such sales success that he demanded a half interest in Ellwood's company. Ellwood refused, Gates organized his own competitive firm, John W. Gates & Company, and eventually their mutual interests led the two to merge their businesses.

Many stories illustrate how Gates earned his nickname, Bet-A-Million Gates. Texans like to think the moniker came from Gates' wagers in their state about the effectiveness of barbed wire. This doubtless contributed to the legend, but Gates was a determined and lifelong gambler. Ellwood claimed that once while riding a train in the rain they had wagered on which drop of water would run down their windowpane quickest. Gates often bet on horse races and engaged in other forms of gambling, but above all he wagered on his own ability to walk

away from any business deal with his position improved.

Gates formed Southern Wire Company in 1881, and with Ellwood, Henry Weil, and Joseph Leiter, in the 1890s also entered the steel business—the supplier of the fundamental source of barbed and other wire. Gates kept himself informed on general business affairs, including Stilwell's effort to build a railroad from Kansas City to the Gulf of Mexico and develop a port in southern Jefferson County. Gates had become acquainted with Stilwell when he sold life insurance. Gates invested $270,000 in Stilwell's financial empire, won a place on the board of directors, and became chairman of a committee to reorganize the company's activities. To learn more about the company, Gates and Stilwell traveled to Port Arthur late in 1899. While there, Gates purchased lots from the Townsite Company and commissioned George Nimmons to construct a colonial mansion for himself and a Pompeian Villa for Ellwood. After that visit, Stilwell's role in the company and authority in southern Jefferson County waned in tandem with Gates' increased influence and power until Stilwell's efforts to found his namesake city became only part of Port Arthur's history.

When the entrepreneurs returned to Chicago, the reorganization committee, run by Gates, forced federal courts to intervene in the

Left: Home of John W. Gates, 2100 Lakeshore, adjacent to the Pompeiian Villa. Dr. Murff F. Bledsoe, prominent Port Arthur surgeon, purchased the home shortly after the death of Mrs. Gates in 1918.
COURTESY OF THE MUSEUM OF THE GULF COAST, PORT ARTHUR, TEXAS.

Below: Mary A. Gates Memorial Hospital, constructed by John W. Gates in memory of his mother at a cost of $25,000. The hospital was located on Lakeshore Drive at the foot of Dallas Avenue. In 1918 Mrs. Gates gave an additional $5,000 for the support of the hospital, and, when she died in 1918, she bequeathed $10,000 to the facility.
COURTESY OF THE MUSEUM OF THE GULF COAST, PORT ARTHUR, TEXAS.

company's business, and eventually Gates succeeded Stilwell as head of the Kansas City, Pittsburg & Gulf Railroad, reorganized as the Kansas City Southern Railroad. Gates son, Charles G. Gates, also took an interest in the development of southern Jefferson County. Soon he controlled the rice mill operation and constructed a powerhouse to generate electricity for the Port Arthur area. After Gates purchased the Port Arthur Channel and Dock Company in 1902, he gained control of the last of Stilwell's assets in the county. Gates regarded his colonial mansion in Port Arthur as his primary home for the remainder of his life, evidenced by the residence there of his wife, although they also had homes in New York and elsewhere. After Gates' death, Mrs. Gates remained a benefactor if not a resident of the area.

OIL

Stilwell's prescience in building a railroad to Port Arthur and shipping facilities there paid off handsomely for Gates. Even before Stilwell

visited the southern part of Jefferson County, other Texans had prospected for "black gold," or oil. Edwin Drake drilled the first American oil well in 1859, and Lynn Taliaferro Barret completed the first well in Texas in Nacogdoches County in 1866. Joseph Cullinan and others brought in wells in Navarro and other counties in Texas in the 1880s. For a decade or more, Patillo Higgins predicted that oil awaited under a slight rise—a salt dome, really—located a few miles south of the business district of Beaumont and fifteen or so miles north of Port Arthur. Higgins named the area Gladys Hill after a young lady in his Sunday School class; the world knows it as Spindletop. There, on January 10, 1901, engineer/driller Anthony Lucas' efforts to develop oil production at Spindletop roared aloft in a gusher that shot upward through the wooden drilling derrick into the sky, then rained crude petroleum on the startled crew.

Spindletop brought Jefferson County, Texas, and the world into the age of oil. In its first year the Spindletop field, with many wells tapping into the subterranean pools of petroleum, surpassed the nation's oil production in Pennsylvania, Ohio, and elsewhere in Texas. The J.M. Guffey Petroleum Company (later Gulf Oil Company), The Texas Oil Company, Hughes Tool Company, and other major oil enterprises got their start at Spindletop, and also participated in expanding oil discovery and production elsewhere in Texas and eventually the world. Oil and petroleum products soon were in demand everywhere because of the rapid development of automobiles with internal combustion engines after the 1890s and the use of oil as a fuel for railroad locomotives instead of coal; the first locomotive powered by oil ran on the Kansas City Southern line from Port Arthur to Lake Charles, Louisiana.

Until deepwater port status was developed for Beaumont and Orange, enabled by dredging channels in the Neches and Sabine rivers to the Port Arthur Canal, all the oil produced at Spindletop was hauled and then piped to Port Arthur for loading aboard ships for transport to eastern American or other destinations. An example was the *Strombus*; she took on sixty thousand barrels of desulphurized oil at the

❖

*Above: Gulf Refinery, August 1929.
Coke stills used in processing
crude oil are visible.*
COURTESY OF THE MUSEUM OF THE GULF COAST,
PORT ARTHUR, TEXAS.

*Left: The Texas Company. Holmes-
Manley stills in the foreground, circa
1930s. Looking eastward with Texas
Company reservoir in the distance
with a view of 25th street.*
COURTESY OF THE PORT ARTHUR PUBLIC LIBRARY
HISTORICAL COLLECTION.

Guffey Company's docks on February 17, 1902. *Strombus'* engines also used oil from Spindletop to spin its own propeller screws. At first, the area shipped oil to refineries located elsewhere; soon, processing of petroleum for gasoline, lubricants, and other usages joined the area's oil boom.

The Texas Company constructed a refinery and eighty-acre tank farm south of Nederland; the city of Port Arthur annexed the area in 1959. The Gulf Oil Company completed two refineries, each capable of processing 62,000 barrels daily. For storage they maintained tanks capable of holding 55,000 barrels each. Guffey and The Port Arthur Channel and Dock Company operated loading docks. Within a short time, Guffey, The Texas Company, and

National Oil and Pipe Line Company delivered crude from Spindletop to one refinery in Beaumont and four refineries in Port Arthur and Nederland. Scores of ships carried the processed oil elsewhere at the average of one vessel per day.

Excursion trains continued to bring prospective businessmen, land purchasers, tourists, and job seekers to Port Arthur. Believers began the First Baptist Church in 1902, and the next year Father Edmund Kelly established St. Mary Catholic Church, which was followed by the founding of Israel Chapel African Methodist Episcopal Church by Frederick Shepherd and the Reverend Napoleon Harris. First Christian Church was established in 1904. The rapid growth, especially in businesses, justified the organization of the Port Arthur Chamber of Commerce in 1903, and a fire department began functioning in 1904; a city police

Above: First National Bank, Proctor Street and Austin Avenue, Port Arthur. Ten men who were the original stockholders organized the bank in 1900 with a capital stock of $50,000 in shares. The officers were President George M. Craig, Vice President, H. H. Beels, and Cashier Frank Cummings. The new office building cost the bank $11,000, plus $1,087.21 for furniture and fixtures.

COURTESY OF THE MUSEUM OF THE GULF COAST, PORT ARTHUR, TEXAS.

Right: Artesian Well. the town of Port Arthur piped its drinking water in a redwood water line from wells in the T. F. McKinney League (now Port Neches Park) to a cement water reservoir in Gilliam Park. These families are celebrating Gates' Day, May 18, 1912, honoring John W. Gates for his contributions to Port Arthur.

COURTESY OF THE PORT ARTHUR PUBLIC LIBRARY HISTORICAL COLLECTION.

Above: Looking Northward at Port Arthur from Pleasure Island, c. 1931
COURTESY OF THE PORT ARTHUR PUBLIC LIBRARY, HISTORICAL COLLECTION.

Left: Pleasure Pier in the 1920s looking northward from Sabine Lake. Note the fan-shaped material placed in the area by dredges maintaining the canal. This dredged material built Pleasure Island as we know it today. Gates' Plaza Hotel is directly in line with the bridge.
COURTESY OF THE PORT ARTHUR PUBLIC LIBRARY, HISTORICAL COLLECTION.

department began two years later. Before 1904 ended, Cosmopolitan Lodge No. 862, A.F. & A.M., the area's first fraternity, began meeting. The *Port Arthur News* became a daily publication, and former Mayor R.H. Woodworth constructed the Woodworth Mansion, or "Rose Hill," which became a city landmark and eventually a public facility. Over 35,000 tons valued at $1.9 million cleared Port Arthur' s docks in 1900; by 1905 exports had exploded to 647 tons, by now mostly petroleum, valued at $14.8 million. The next year Congress approved the designation of Port Arthur as an official port of entry and assumed authority and responsibility for the ship canal, and Russell Dunn became the first customs collector there; L.E. Wood also became the first harbormaster of the port. Within little more than a decade, Port Arthur joined the ranks of the nation's busiest ports in tonnage, mostly petroleum. In separate legislation, Congress also authorized dredging of the Sabine and Neches rivers from Orange and Beaumont to a connection with Port Arthur's ship channel, to make those cities deep-water ports as well. The first barge from Orange carried lumber to the Texas Company Docks; wagons hauled this essential building material to various company, lumberyard, and construction sites.

The Texas Company purchased Central Asphalt & Refining Company in Port Neches, then still known as Grigsby's Bluff. To replace Hotel Sabine, which burned in 1903, as Port Arthur's central meeting facility and primary quality host, Gates built The Plaza Hotel. He purchased Stilwell's experimental farm and renamed it Port Arthur Nurseries, and from it, donated 1,000 eucalyptus trees to decorate the city's boulevards. Gates Model Farm, located on North Procter Street, produced and marketed milk and milk products, eggs, figs, oranges, grapefruit—and all those eucalyptus trees. Gates was a major player in the founding of Mary Gates Memorial Hospital, named in honor of Gates' mother, and of Port Arthur Business College.

By 1908 Port Arthur claimed over 8,000 residents and old and new communities in the southern part of Jefferson County prospered as well. Sabine Pass lost most of its shipping prominence to Port Arthur, but Sun Oil Company constructed loading docks in that coastal area after the discovery of oil at Spindletop; the docks remained in service until 1927. Port Arthur annexed the area in 1978, but Sabine Pass continued as a distinct community, and as late as 1984, when the *Texas Almanac* reported population figures separately from Port Arthur, approximately 1,500 lived there.

Sun Oil, The Texas Company, and Pure (later Union) Oil Company played major roles in the development of Nederland by establishing major terminals or refineries there. Nederland enjoyed rail transportation to Port Arthur and Beaumont via an interurban service. The *Mid-County Chronicle* began publishing in Nederland in 1930. The population of Nederland gradually increased to more than 16,000 by 2000 through natural growth and development and the city's function as a bedroom community for Port Arthur and Beaumont.

The Griffing brothers laid out the community of Groves, originally called Peach Groves and later The Groves, on a tract they acquired from Gates. Like a great deal of southern Jefferson County, Groves became an industrial-residential city, especially after the Atlantic Oil Company established a refinery near there on a site later occupied by BASF, and by the end of the century claimed over 16,000 residents.

John Warne Gates died on August 9, 1911, while in Paris. When the news reached Port Arthur, flags were struck to half-mast and local industries he owned and/or controlled shut down for the day. City and Chamber officials recruited a delegation to attend the funeral in New York City, businesses in Port Arthur closed in memoriam on that date, and 2,000 people gathered in a memorial service on the lawn of the Plaza Hotel, a facility opened in 1909 by Gates. A year later the community observed its first annual Gates Day, a commemorative celebration of Gates' short but significant association with Port Arthur and southern Jefferson County; Gates Day observance ceased in 1920 because of the request from the Gates family. The first celebration featured a train ride to Port Neches and a picnic for all Port Arthur children.

Port Neches also became the source of Port Arthur's fresh water. Water from two artesian wells surged through eight miles of mains constructed of redwood to Port Arthur to supply 1.3 million gallons daily. The wells were purchased through a $460,000 bond issue, and the project became operational on June 12, 1913. Additional development could be seen in the introduction of a regular interurban rail line between Port Arthur and Beaumont. By 1914 the volume of tonnage shipped through Port Arthur raised it to the rank of fourteenth in the nation. Its population had reached 12,600 people, served by a public library, electric and gas utilities, two newspapers, a booming petroleum business constantly in need of labor—and unwarranted confidence that the city enjoyed "absolute protection from damage by Gulf Storms."

Future hurricanes proved that assumption fatally wrong, but in 1914 the immediate "storm" came from across the Atlantic Ocean, where German powers fought against Britain and France. Each side had additional alliances, so the Great War, the name for this confrontation until after 1941, has been known since as World War I. Europeans fought for three years, 1914-1917, before the United States joined them as a belligerent against Germany, but southern Jefferson County experienced the effects of the war long before then. Additional demand for petroleum products in Europe due to war's acceleration of consumption called for increased production at area refineries and additional shipping. Refineries in Jefferson County produced more than one million gallons of fuel weekly during the war.

Port Arthur citizens got to see some of the consequences of war when the oil tanker *Gulflight* steamed into their port in May 1915, showing damage sustained in the Mediterranean Sea from a German submarine. In 1917 a German sub also took down the British steamer *Saxonian*, filled with oil shipped from Port Arthur. Sobered by the reality of war, Gulf Refining, The Texas Company, and Port Arthur Canal and Dock Company closed their facilities to visitors and issued identification badges to employees. With more than twenty-eight hundred people working the Gulf refinery alone, this proved quite a change and a task. Preparation for the war, declared by Congress in April 1917, included the organization of

Alfred Small minding the store with the help of his first grandson, Howard Dean Smith, in this family-owned store on Port Arthur's West side. Also in the photo on the left are Logan Smith and Leroy Smith.

COURTESY OF THE MUSEUM OF THE GULF COAST, PORT ARTHUR, TEXAS.

817
818
GOODHUE
HOTEL
COFFEE SHOP
BARBER SHOP

Company A, Texas Engineers, 36th Infantry Division, National Guard, commanded by Captain James G.L. Howard; other officers included Lieutenants Richard B. Dunbar and Richard A. McClanaghan.

Allied demands and our own military necessity made for serious shortages during World War I. Sugar and flour, staples in most south Jefferson kitchens, disappeared with use and proved difficult to replace. The War Garden Association assisted area residents, including those without yards who could use vacant lots and even some public parks, to supplement their tables with fresh produce. And the impact of war was evident in the decision to change the name of German Avenue to Pershing Avenue in Port Arthur. Worse than war, at least locally, was an epidemic of Spanish influenza that swept the area in 1918. To prevent additional communication of the disease, Port Arthur's mayor closed theatres and places of amusement, schools—even churches—until the danger passed.

Despite the tensions of war and disease, people continued to be joiners. A Rotary Club was organized in Port Arthur in 1915, followed by a Lions Cub in 1917. The next year Local 23 received its charter from the American Federation of Labor's Oil Workers International Union, and the Reverend Otho Morris, pastor of First Methodist Church, organized the first Boy Scout troop in the city. Local 1175 of the International Longshoreman's Association began in 1921.

In 1920, Port Arthur's population figures stood at 22,276. The value of annual exports through its port exceeded $13 million, and the city provided several new schools for its young scholars, including Lincoln School for Negroes. Residents of the area celebrated being "first" at many things; in 1921, Port Arthur's citizens boasted of hosting the first all-woman jury in Texas. The case involved a woman accused of assault, and when an all-male jury voted for acquittal, the irritated judge dismissed the men and impaneled a new, all-woman, jury. Jury Number 2 required only four minutes to return a guilty verdict, and an observer said they even used "their vanity cases" during some of that time. Port Arthur also scored another "first" in 1926 when school superintendent George Sims added a twelfth grade to the public school curriculum. Soon all schools in Texas followed that lead.

Southern Jefferson County, like the rest of America, witnessed significant social change after the war. Returning servicemen sometimes found their old jobs filled by women or minorities who did not want to return to second-class economic citizenship. During that decade many women shortened their skirts, bobbed their hair, and behaved in a more liberated fashion. Traditionalism fought back through the dismissal of all schoolteachers who had adopted the "flapper-style," and in a solemn march by the Knights of the Ku Klux Klan down Procter Street carrying an American flag and a fiery cross.

Atlantic Refining Company joined Gulf and The Texas Company as a member of the area's industrial community in 1923; Fina eventually succeeded Atlantic on that site (now BASF). Additional growth could be seen in the completion in 1925 of a "Hug-The-Coast" road linking Port Arthur and Galveston via a ferry at the end of Bolivar Peninsula. It made use of a right of way already established from Port Arthur to McFaddin Beach, and United States Post Road, a trail along the coast dating back to the Civil War. When the road opened, the ferry to Galveston made only three round-trips per day and cost $1 for an automobile. A road to Orange, again with a ferry across the Sabine River, also was completed, and surveyors busily worked westward to extend the Intracoastal Canal. In addition, in fulfillment of a decision by the

Opposite: Beaumont capitalist Forrest Goodhue built the ten-story Goodhue Hotel in Port Arthur at a cost of $500,000 in 1929. After serving the entire region for almost sixty-one years, it was imploded by the City of Port Arthur in August 1990. The Goodhue debris was placed along the Sabine-Neches waterway to protect Pleasure Island from further erosion.
COURTESY OF THE MUSEUM OF THE GULF COAST, PORT ARTHUR, TEXAS.

Below: Port Arthur citizens celebrate Armistice Day in 1920 in front of the Federal Building on Austin Avenue and Fifth Street.
COURTESY OF THE MUSEUM OF THE GULF COAST, PORT ARTHUR, TEXAS.

Austin Avenue and Fifth Street flooded by a storm surge. A hurricane hit Port Arthur in August 1915 and flooded the town for almost three weeks. The Federal Building, 320 Austin Avenue, can be seen on extreme right. A child was born in the building during the storm and was named "Federal Building" by his parents, Mr. and Mrs. J. M. Wright. Construction of the building was completed in 1912 at a cost of $120,300. The offices of the government's postal, customs, immigration, quarantine, agriculture, public health, and recruiting services, and the Port Arthur office of the United States Weather Bureau were housed in the building.

Interstate Commerce Commission, Kansas City Southern's monopoly in south Jefferson County ended, and its facilities opened to other carriers.

Arthur Stilwell, founder of Port Arthur and other communities in the south Jefferson County area, died in New York. Just how completely John W. Gates has eclipsed Stilwell in the area could be seen in its response to his passing. Instead of sending a delegation to the funeral, city officials sent their condolences and a spray of flowers seven feet tall and three feet wide. Perhaps too much time had passed, and too many new residents had no knowledge or memory of his early efforts.

Still, Stilwell had launched his namesake city well, and its development continued through the 1920s. With state cooperation, the Corps of Engineers supervised the construction of a nine-foot seawall around the city to protect it from the occasionally angry waters of Lake Sabine, and also a widening of the ship channel. The seawall, plus a new bridge to Pleasure Island, was completed in October 1931. The Vaughn Hotel (later the Sabine), the Goodhue Hotel, and Eddingston Court, the city's first apartment complex located on Procter Street, opened in the summer of 1929. The most outstanding feature of the Court was a wall decorated with over six thousand conch shells from the Cayman Islands. St. Mary Hospital, a successor institution to Mary Gates Memorial Hospital,

opened on Ninth Avenue. The Port Arthur Rose Garden Club established a municipal garden and 154 raised beds along Lakeshore Drive and encouraged the planting of thousands of rose bushes throughout the area. A sadder reminder of the past occurred in May 1930, when the remains of Rudolph Lambert, a soldier and the first casualty of World War I from Port Arthur, came home for burial. The American Legion Post there was named in Lambert's honor. The next year, Port Arthur's list of "firsts" expanded when Governor Ross Sterling signed legislation allowing the location of a sub-courthouse in the city because its population had reached fifty thousand, almost as many as the county seat, Beaumont.

In just over three decades, the villages of south Jefferson County had grown dramatically. Sabine Pass continued to serve as eastern Texas' outlet to the sea and trade with the world; Nederland and Port Neches shared Port Arthur's progress in petroleum and related industries, and that city had become the seventh busiest port in tonnage in the United States. The area had endured and survived hurricanes, a world war, and economic consequences and social changes produced by such experiences. New challenges just ahead in Depression and war, and social changes would demand leadership and grit, without a Stilwell or a Gates to guide the way.

CHAPTER **IV**

DEPRESSION, WAR & SOCIAL CHANGE

Residents of southern Jefferson County entered the 1930s, and the Great Depression, better prepared than a great many other Texans and Americans. The loss of international markets after World War I produced an agricultural slump in the South, especially in cotton production, but Jefferson County did not depend on cotton, as did many other counties in East and South Texas. Also, discoveries in the oil industry, first at Spindletop, then elsewhere in the county and state, the spectacular EasTex field near Kilgore, and resulting construction and operation of pipelines and refineries, produced a recurring boom in the county.

Years later, many people chuckled, "We never knew when the Depression started," meaning that the crash on Wall Street in October 1929 had no immediate effect on them because they owned no stocks or bonds or they enjoyed steady work in the oil fields and refineries. Belts had to be tightened, of course—for a time the cities paid employees in scrip rather than their regular checks—but Jefferson County got through the Depression with less stress than many other parts of the nation, and the population even increased, because many East Texans and southwest Louisianans moved to the

❖

Texaco Island. Located at the junction of the Sabine-Neches Canal and the Port Arthur canal, September 9, 1953. The grain elevator built by Arthur Stilwell in 1897 is in the lower center of the image. The Kansas City Southern Railway yards are next to grain elevator.

COURTESY OF THE PORT ARTHUR PUBLIC LIBRARY, HISTORICAL COLLECTION.

The Port Arthur Board of Education, Port Arthur Independent School District in 1935. Members are, left to right, front row: George Sims, Superintendent, Ms. Joe Harle, A.M. McAfee, President, Mrs. Carl White, Calder Yates; back row: Perry LaGrone, E. P. Baker, F. D. Austin, and L. B. Abbey, secretary.

area in anticipation of work producing, refining, or shipping petroleum.

Port Arthur and Beaumont enjoyed a visit from the U.S. frigate *Constitution*, "Old Ironsides," early in 1932. Thousands of residents of the county turned out to visit this surviving artifact of the United States' war with England, 1812-1815, over a century earlier. Despite such distractions, the area experienced various ups and downs in the 1930s. For example, the City of Port Arthur laid off approximately fifty of 218 employees—nearly one quarter of its labor force—and First National Bank survived a "run" only with the assistance of a $750,000 advance from the Federal Reserve System delivered by airplane. On the other hand, Radio Station KPAC, with Port Arthur College as licensee, debuted, and Bruno Schultz founded the Gulfport Shipbuilding Corporation despite the national economic depression. Interurban service to Beaumont, operational since 1931, ceased, mostly because of competition from automobiles, buses, and trucks; in its nearly two decades of service the interurban transported 9,077,472 passengers, a total of 6,624,757 miles. On the other hand, work began on a bridge at Dryden's Ferry across the Neches River connecting the Port Arthur-Orange highway, and Port Arthur's Hunting Club—a leisure activity demonstrating discretionary income expenditure—began operating with members from its namesake city, Nederland, Beaumont, and Houston. A new community located two

miles west of Nederland and midway between Port Arthur and Beaumont—and so named Beauxart Gardens—was platted and soon claimed a population of fifty families.

Port Arthur's schools took on different roles when Thomas Jefferson Junior High School was changed to the town's primary public high school, and the old high school campus on Lakeshore Drive became Woodrow Wilson Junior High.

Additional evidence of the impact of the Depression could be seen in City Manager Robert Cooper's disclosure that taxpayers had fallen behind in property tax payments by approximately $500,000, which he called an "astounding figure." And in 1935, the first project of the New Deal agency known as the Works Progress Administration in Port Arthur, the construction of a sub-county courthouse, began. The project employed fifty-one men for three-quarters of a year.

In 1937, Port Arthur's City Commission held a contest to determine a slogan that would best capture the essence of the city. Commissioners invited the public to submit recommendations and, out of 423 responses, selected "We Oil The World," the recommendation of Mrs. Hollie D. Sudduth. The slogan represented the vocational focus, directly or indirectly, of every citizen of the city and much of the southern portion of the county as well.

Improvements to Dick Dowling Park at Sabine Pass, especially the addition of a statue of Dowling, attracted more tourists, Port Arthur Lines began operating a regular city bus schedule—rides cost five cents—and airmail service began in December 1937. But the most significant Depression era advancement in the area occurred on September 8, 1938, with the opening of the Rainbow Bridge at Dryden's Crossing, making possible continuous automotive transportation between south Jefferson County and Orange. The two-lane bridge cost $2.75 million and connected literally hundreds of thousands of people who commuted daily to industrial employment, leisure activities, or family visits. Called a "rainbow" because it rose 176 feet above the river to allow passage of ocean vessels upriver to Beaumont, availability of the bridge connected the southern portion of the county to Orange, and then on to Lake Charles and New Orleans, Louisiana. The dedication ceremony featured presentations by Texas Governor James V. Allred and Louisiana Attorney General Gaston Poerterie; each held one end of the ribbon so Miss Mary Elizabeth Mills, daughter of a Jefferson County Commissioner H. O. Mills, could cut the ribbon.

Bert L. Barrett of Beaumont became a typical user of the Rainbow Bridge after he went to work at Dupont's Sabine River plant in Orange late in the 1940s. Barrett and three others in his car pool crossed the Rainbow Bridge twice daily, going to and from the Dupont plant every working day for twenty-seven years. The bridge shortened transit time considerably because commuters did not have to wait for the ferry or drive to Orange via Beaumont, almost twice the distance between South Jefferson County and Orange.

The world returned to war in the 1930s because of the aggression of Germany and Italy, led by Adolph Hitler and Benito Mussolini, and Japan, where the emperor had become a figurehead in a country then in the hands of militarists. England and France went to war with Germany in 1938 over the German invasion of Poland, and increased demand for petroleum products stimulated the refining and shipping industries located in Port Neches and Port Arthur. The Burke-Wadsworth Act instituted the first peacetime military draft in American history, drawing several young men into military assignments. War found the United States on December 7, 1941, when Japanese aerial forces launched from aircraft carriers, "suddenly and deliberately" attacked the American Navy, Marine, Army, and Army Air Corps in Hawaii, especially in Pearl Harbor, while the majority of the nation's Pacific Fleet, moored there, awoke on what had been, until the attack, a leisurely Sunday morning. President Franklin D. Roosevelt denounced Japan's attack, saying the day would live in "infamy." Congress declared war on Japan on December 8, and two days later on Germany and Italy because those nations honored their Axis Powers agreement and declared war on the United States.

Because of the draft and Roosevelt's efforts to aid England and France since 1938, America was slightly more prepared for war than the nation had been in 1917. The Army and Navy already had begun the expansion that ultimately grew into a thirteen-million person force; the industrial base had matured, and the people knew instantly, on December 7, what was at stake in the war. Like Americans everywhere, residents of south Jefferson County made sacrifices because "there's a war on, don't you know?" The Office of Price Administration administered rationing of such staples as sugar and coffee, which required ration stamps as well as money to purchase, and meat, which required "red points," or dime-sized plastic disks. Gasoline and shoes, also joined the ration list. No autos were manufactured for civilians; instead, car makers concentrated on jeeps and tanks and semi trucks and airplanes. Victory gardens appeared in many back yards, and hordes of men—then women—not in a military service, flocked to jobs in coastal shipyards, refineries, and chemical plants, such as those that produced synthetic rubber. Banners with stars appeared in windows with each star representing a household member in the service; a gold star meant that soldier or sailor from that home had been a casualty of the war. Housing was as scarce as new tires, and many wartime romances resulted in hasty marriages.

COURTESY OF THE MUSEUM OF THE GULF COAST, PORT ARTHUR, TEXAS.

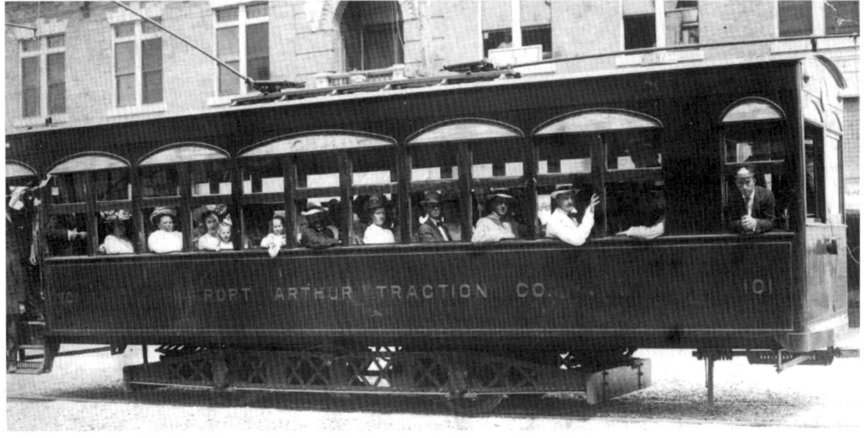

The reality of war came home with news that sailor Joseph George Koenig of Port Arthur, aged nineteen, had been killed in the attack on Pearl Harbor. Over 1,000 men and a few women from Port Arthur joined military services after Pearl Harbor, many more were drafted, and Port Arthur's mayor, Dr. L. C. Heare, resigned to accept a commission in the Army. The first synthetic rubber was produced by B. F. Goodrich with products supplied by Neches Butane Company. Communities staged "black outs," or

drills to prepare for air attacks, and sighting of German submarines just off the coast made south county citizens uneasy. Churches opened and businesses closed on June 6, 1944, when news of the Allied invasion at Normandy reached the county, so worshipers could pray for the success of our servicemen, and, at the request of the U.S. Army, Port Arthur's "red-light district" closed, at least temporarily, displacing sixty-nine practitioners of the world's "oldest profession." Everyone in Jefferson County learned of the heroism of Sergeant Lucian Adams, Jefferson County's only winner of the Congressional Medal of Honor during the war; Sergeant Adams was a member of the 30th Infantry, 3rd Division. Eventually a street and a park were named in his honor.

The postwar era brought new challenges, such as the reemployment of returning service persons. The G.I. Bill of Rights enabled educational expansion for a generation by paying for veterans to enroll in vocational schools or colleges. In 1948, Port Arthur Mayor James W. Long led the community in celebration of its Golden Jubilee, or fiftieth anniversary, and Texas Lieutenant Governor Allan Shivers, who had grown up in Port Arthur, became governor of Texas when Governor Beauford Jester died. The release of wartime commitments also made

labor strife more probable; for example, in 1950, workers struck the Texas Company for 115 days.

Change came to the south county area more rapidly in the postwar world. Dorothy Ingram became the first black female school principal in Port Arthur, albeit in a segregated school. More annual festivals, such as CavOILcade, began in 1953 and, in June 1957, the entire county sustained significant damage from Hurricane Audrey. The tropical hurricane struck heaviest in Cameron Parish, Louisiana, where most of the storm's 500 or so fatalities occurred, then swept up the Sabine River. The storm surge extended twenty-five miles inland, and southern Jefferson County received wind gusts of 100 miles per hour, causing significant structural damage and power outages.

A storm of a different kind struck Jefferson County in 1961 when Representative Tom James of Dallas, leader of the State Investigating Committee (also known as the James Commission), held hearings in Beaumont on corruption in the county. The hearings produced testimony incriminating popular Sheriff Charley Meyer, police chiefs of cities in the county and members of their police forces, and other public officials. The investigation revealed that the entire county was "wide open"

LUCIAN ADAMS

Lucian Adams, winner of the Congressional Medal of Honor for action "above and beyond the call of duty" near St. Die, France, on October 28, 1944, which was one week past his twenty-second birthday.

Adams, a native of Port Arthur and a graduate of Franklin Junior High and Port Arthur High School, entered the army soon after his graduation. He served first in the Casino Campaign in Italy, where he received the Purple Heart and Bronze Star for gallantry.

Later, in France, Staff Sergeant Adams, a member of the 30th Infantry Division, so distinguished himself under fire at St. Die that he received the Congressional Medal of Honor. The citation reads, in part:

When his company was stopped in its effort to drive through the Mortagne Forest to reopen the supply line to the isolated third battalion, S/Sgt. Adams braved the concentrated fire of machineguns in a lone assault on a force of German troops. Although his company had progressed less than 10 yards and had lost 3 killed and 6 wounded, S/Sgt. Adams charged forward dodging from tree to tree firing a borrowed BAR from the hip. Despite intense machinegun fire which the enemy directed at him and rifle grenades which struck the trees over his head showering him with broken twigs and branches, S/Sgt. Adams made his way to within 10 yards of the closest machinegun and killed the gunner with a hand grenade. An enemy soldier threw hand grenades at him from a position only 10 yards distant; however, S/Sgt. Adams dispatched him with a single burst of BAR fire. Charging into the vortex of the enemy fire, he killed another machinegunner at 15 yards range with a hand grenade and forced the surrender of 2 supporting infantrymen. Although the remainder of the German group concentrated the full force of its automatic weapons fire in a desperate effort to knock him out, he proceeded through the woods to find and exterminate 5 more of the enemy. Finally, when the third German machinegun opened up on him at a range of 20 yards, S/Sgt. Adams killed the gunner with BAR fire. In the course of the action, he personally killed 9 Germans, eliminated 3 enemy machineguns, vanquished a specialized force which was armed with automatic weapons and grenade launchers, cleared the woods of hostile elements, and reopened the severed supply lines to the assault companies of his battalion.

Sergeant Adams received the Medal of Honor on March 29, 1945. After the war he worked for the Veterans Administration until retirement in 1986. He died on March 31, 2003.

A grateful city renamed Aurora Park in Port Arthur Lucian Adams Field, and a portion of 61st Street was renamed in his honor. A bust of Adams is on display in the Museum of the Gulf Coast.

Lucian Adams, Congressional Medal of Honor recipient "for conspicuous gallantry and intrepidity at risk of life above and beyond the call of duty on October 28, 1944, near St. Die, France." When Adams' assault on the Germans was over, he had single-handedly eliminated a specialized German unit armed with automatic weapons and grenade launchers, killed nine enemy soldiers, and enabled the U.S. Army 30th Infantry to reopen supply lines for the Third Battalion. President Ronald Reagan congratulates Adams at a reunion of Medal of Honor recipients in Washington.

COURTESY OF THE MUSEUM OF THE GULF COAST, PORT ARTHUR, TEXAS.

Former Texas Governor Allan Shivers and his wife, Marialice, admiring the Texas Historical Marker in front of the Shivers Museum in Woodville, Texas. Shivers was born in Lufkin, and his family moved to Port Arthur when he was 16. He graduated from Thomas Jefferson High School, Port Arthur College, and law school. Shivers was elected Lt. Governor of Texas in 1946 and served as Governor 1949-1957.

to illegal gambling, alcohol violations, and prostitution, all tolerated by some law enforcement officers, prosecutors, and judges because of payoffs. Stories of Beaumont's notorious Dixie Hotel, operated on Crockett Street by Rita Ainsworth, and Meyer, led the news, but Grace Woodyard's and Marcella Chadwell's red-light houses, two of fourteen known prostitution parlors in Port Arthur, also attracted the attention of media and the James Commission. As a result, Meyer, the district attorney, and the police chiefs lost their jobs, and Ainsworth, Woodyard, and Chadwell temporarily went out of business. Such illegal activities resumed, of course, but not so blatantly or so openly in conjunction with law enforcement.

The Supreme Court ordered racial integration of public education "with all deliberate speed" in May 1954, but schools operated by Port Arthur Independent School District did not begin integration until 1961, and then only for kindergarten and first grade under a plan that advanced one grade each year. School faculties and staffs integrated in 1965, and the United States Department of Justice ordered abandonment of the one grade per year plan in favor of complete integration. For generations, the Thomas Jefferson Yellow Jackets (whites) and Lincoln Bumblebees (African Americans) were perennial high school district champions and play-off threats; both won state championships in football or basketball. Pride and reluctance to give up such traditions doubtless worked some hardship on the students involved, but ultimately integrated athletics helped ease the inevitable tension of court-ordered integration. In the meantime, in the area's parochial education, Bishop Byrne Catholic High School occupied new facilities on Ninth Avenue after Sacred Heart, Saint Mary, and Saint James high schools merged.

The 1960s were also a time of renewal. In 1967, the Corps of Engineers contracted with Coastal Construction Company to build a new, $8.5 million bridge to Pleasure Island—dedicated in 1970 as the Martin Luther King, Jr. Bridge—and two years later citizens celebrated the opening of a new Port of Port Arthur, financed by a $9 million bond issue. On the other hand, the Kansas City Southern, which had brought many of the first generation of south Jefferson countians to help fulfill Arthur Stilwell's dream, ceased passenger service to the area. The railroad's depot and the old bridge to

"Babe" Didrikson Zaharias, July 1948. She was recognized as the greatest female athlete in the world.
COURTESY OF THE MUSEUM OF THE GULF COAST, PORT ARTHUR, TEXAS.

Pleasure Island were demolished in 1968. Port Arthur's public transit service also ceased operating in 1970, partly due to a driver's strike and because of denial of a request for a subsidy increase.

Trustees for Port Arthur College agreed to merge with Lamar University, headquartered in Beaumont, and became Lamar University—Port Arthur. The new arrangement began operating in

HARRY CHOATES

Harry Henry Choates was born in Louisiana, on December 26, 1922, and moved to Port Arthur with his mother in the 1930s. Choates had no formal education, preferring the streets and listening to recordings played on jukeboxes in bars. By the age of twelve he played the fiddle for tips, and eventually learned to play the accordion, standard guitar, and steel guitar as well.

Early in the 1940s Choates played with Cajun music bands led by Leo Soileau and Leroy ("Happy Fats") LeBlanc, and in 1946 wrote and recorded *Jole Blon*, which became a theme song for Cajun music. Choates' high-pitched "aaiee" vocal call became his signature. An alcoholic, Choate sold the rights to *Jole Blon* for $100 and a bottle of whiskey.

Choates' band, The Melody Boys, played in bars and honky tonks and recorded dozens of songs, though none achieved the success of *Jole Blon*. He died in jail in Austin, Texas, on July 17, 1951.

Choates is credited with merging traditional Cajun music with country and swing styles, and the popularization of accordion and fiddle sounds associated with Cajun music.

Harry Choates, known as the "Godfather of Cajun Music." Choates wrote and played Jole Blon, *known as the Cajun national anthem.*

established facilities in 1975 with 385 students; Sam Monroe served as president. In 1999 the Texas legislature designated the institution as Lamar State College—Port Arthur, a separate entity under the Texas State University System's Board of Regents. By 1990 enrollment exceeded 2,000 students and approached 3,000 students by the end of that decade.

South Jefferson County hosted the most heavily unionized labor force in Texas for much of the twentieth century. Locals of both Congress of Industrial Organizations and American Federation of Labor affiliates constituted a majority of the work force in oil, chemical, and other industrial plants. Labor strikes occurred periodically, sometimes as jurisdictional disputes between CIO and AFL locals and always to obtain better wages and working conditions for members. Long-time residents remember particularly violent labor unrest in the 1950s, but all strikes generated hard and hurt feelings for both management and labor. In 1975 and 1979, literally thousands of workers were either on strike or locked out of the Gulf and Texas Company refineries. In contrast, by the end of the century, area refineries and chemical plants began laying off workers no longer needed because of automation or because much of the work had shifted to other areas.

The downsizing of industry resulted in closings for many main-street retail businesses dependent on customers with good paying industrial jobs for their own success. The development of shopping malls and convenience stores also drew customers from more traditional, downtown merchants. Too, even when industries continued to operate with reduced labor forces, they did so under new management. For example, U.S. Industrial Chemicals bought out ARCO and Chevron USA bought Gulf in rounds of corporate raids, take overs and mergers that continued into the twenty-first century; Gulf eventually became Clark and later Valero, an example of Wall Street play common at the end of the millennium and the beginning of the twenty-first century. Unemployment reached twenty-five percent in Port Arthur in 1986, and the city's population dropped from a high of more than 66,000 in 1960s to approximately 58,000 in 1990.

Changes were apparent in leadership and in the appearance of the area. In 1990, Cornelius Boganey became the first African American city manager of Port Arthur, the same year Mary Ellen Summerlin was selected the city's first woman mayor. Raymond Johnson, another African American, became president of the Port of Port Arthur. On the other hand, workers imploded the Goodhue Hotel, dark for twenty years, and constructed new federal and state prisons in the central portion of Jefferson County near Nederland and Port Neches, providing needed employment

❖

Above: Mrs. Leola King and W. J. Dickerson admire a billboard recognizing Port Arthur's selection as one of ten cities in the United States to win the coveted All-American City Award in 1973. This recognition was made possible by municipal improvements made in the preceding ten years.

COURTESY OF THE MUSEUM OF THE GULF COAST, PORT ARTHUR, TEXAS.

Below: W. Sam Monroe, president of Lamar University Port Arthur, now Lamar State College–Port Arthur, 1975.

COURTESY OF THE PORT ARTHUR PUBLIC LIBRARY, HISTORICAL COLLECTION.

for many residents in the construction and operation of the facilities.

In February 1993, the first Mardi Gras of Southeast Texas took over downtown Port Arthur, and an estimated 100,000 people lined Procter Street for parades and other events; within five years direct participants operated twelve "krewes," and attendees had increased to over 250,000 people.

Southern Jefferson County, especially Port Arthur completed its first century in the 1990s. Some areas, such as Sabine Pass, though older,

TEX RITTER

Tex Ritter, born Maurice Woodward Ritter on January 12, 1905, in Murvaul, Panola County, moved to Nederland and was graduated from South Park High School in 1922. He attended law school at the University of Texas for one year, but, influenced by folklorists J. Frank Dobie and John Lomax, Ritter became more interested in Western music.

Ritter began singing on Radio Station KPRC in Houston in 1929, and by 1931 had joined the Theatre Guild in New York, where he played a role in *Green Grow The Lilacs*, which later became the musical *Oklahoma!* He starred in a Western musical radio program titled *The Lone Star Rangers*, one of the first to be broadcast in New York, then moved to Hollywood in 1936 to perform in Western movies. For six years Ritter was one of Hollywood's top ten moneymaking stars.

Ritter's best-known musical recordings were *High Noon*, released in 1952 in conjunction with a major motion picture of the same name, and *The Wayward Wind*, released in 1956. He appeared on the Grand Ole Opry and became the fifth inductee in the Country Music Hall of Fame in 1964.

Ritter married Dorothy Fay Southworth in 1941 and they were the parents of two sons, including John Ritter, star of television series and movies.

Ritter died in Nashville, Tennessee, on January 1, 1974. Funeral services were held in Nederland, and he was interred in Oak Bluff Memorial Park in Port Neches.

just barely hung on to community status; others, such as Nederland, Port Neches, and Groves, were younger but strong and growing; some, such as Port Acres and Griffing, became part of Port Arthur when residents of Griffing Park and Port Arthur voted approval. Their cumulative population easily exceeded one hundred thousand people and territorial boundaries, and actual settlement patterns had become busy streets; residents of what some considered Nederland actually lived in Port Arthur's jurisdiction. Modern hospitals and professionals provided advanced medical services, and churches by the score attempted to address spiritual and moral needs. Retail business from "Big Box" to Mom-and-Pop enterprises—though now Mom and Pop were as likely to be Vietnamese, Middle Eastern, or other Asians—some in malls and some in stand-alone structures, offered the food and fiber upon which an urbanized people must depend. The color and face of the community had changed, especially in government and education, and labor unions no longer wielded as much influence as in an earlier time; business itself, especially heavy industry, had a more corporate, less local focus.

Left: Members of the Port Arthur Centennial Commission pose for publicity photograph in front of the historical home, Pompeiian Villa. From left to right they are: Ben and Corrine Jones, Dorothy Ingram, Bob Brammer, Hazel Baron, Dave Smith, Yvonne Sutherlin, Dub Brown, Mayor Bob Morgan, Verna Rutherford, Ed Kestler, Edith Huber-Logsdon, Lonnie Logsdon, and Sissy Wood.
COURTESY OF WINSTON B. LEWIS, PHOTOGRAPHER, ORANGE, TEXAS.

Below: The winners in the 1954 CavOILcade hat contest.
COURTESY OF THE MUSEUM OF THE GULF COAST, PORT ARTHUR, TEXAS.

J. P. RICHARDSON

Jiles Perry Richardson, or the Big Bopper to the rock-and-roll generation, was born in Sabine Pass, Texas, on October 24, 1930. Richardson attended high school in Beaumont after his family moved there, and he also began pre-law studies at Lamar College while working part time at Radio Station KTRM.

In 1949 Richardson opted for full-time employment with the radio station and over the next few years worked as an announcer and disk jockey in various time slots, beginning with a late morning "Dishwasher's Serenade," late afternoon, and eventually 9:00 p.m. until midnight. Except for two years in the U.S. Army, Richardson worked at KTRM for the remainder of his life; in 1957 he set a record for most continuous on-air broadcasting at five days, two hours, and eight minutes, for which he earned $746 overtime compensation.

Richardson composed songs for country music entertainers George Jones and Johnny Preston, and in 1958, as the Big Bopper, recorded *Chantilly Lace*, which remained in the Top 40 for twenty-two weeks and is a classic song today. Because of its success, Richardson joined Buddy Holly and Ritchie Vallens on a tour. Richardson, Holly, and Vallens, died on February 3, 1959, when their chartered airplane went down en route to Fargo, North Dakota. In a later recording, artist Don McLean referred to this event in his anthem, *The Day The Music Died*.

J. P. Richardson, Jr., "The Big Bopper,"
wrote the hits Chantilly Lace *and*
Running Bear.

Like Charles Dickens' earlier tale of two (or more) cities, the south Jefferson County's centennial was the best of times for some, the worst of time for others. A century after their impact, some citizens had read of Arthur Stilwell and John Warne Gates in commemorative issues of the Port Arthur News or other regional papers, but not all knew of the rancor between them, or which was the visionary and which the practical developer. Just about everyone in the area, dwelling as they did amongst oil refineries and chemical plants and close to the Gulf of Mexico, had an awareness of the important role producing and refining petroleum and shipping its products to markets throughout the world had played in the economic development of the area. They were aware, too, of the multicultural rainbow

LEE HAZELWOOD

Barton Lee Hazelwood was born in Mannford, Oklahoma, on July 9, 1929. His father, Gabe Hazelwood, a wildcatter and dance promoter, moved his family frequently, so Hazelwood attended high school in Port Neches. Hazelwood's association with country music, including meeting Bob Wills when he was still an infant, and his itinerant lifestyle, began with this parental influence.

Hazelwood briefly attended Lon Morris College before serving in the Army in Korea and Alaska as a member of the Fourth Army Division Band. He married high school sweetheart Naomi Shackleford in ceremonies held in Port Neches.

Hazelwood attended Spears Broadcasting School in Los Angeles, then became a disc jockey for Station KCKY in Coolidge, Arizona, the first of many such employments before he became a successful performer, music writer and producer, and foreign traveler. There he met Al Casey and Duane Eddy, who also became famous musical performers.

Hazelwood developed his unique "twangy guitar" sound on the way to becoming a headliner in the 1960s. He wrote and arranged musical scores, performed in movies, and produced records, most memorably *These Boots Are Made For Walking* with Nancy Sinatra in 1966.

Thereafter Hazelwood lived and worked mostly in Sweden, England, France, and Spain. He died on August 4, 2007.

JANIS JOPLIN

Janis Joplin was born in Port Arthur on January 19, 1943. Joplin's father worked as a supervisor for the Texas Company, and she grew up singing in a church choir. Joplin attended Thomas Jefferson High School at the same time Jimmy Johnson was a student there, and Johnson claimed to have given her the nickname "beat weeds."

After an unhappy high school experience, Joplin enrolled in the University of Texas, Austin, but did not graduate. Instead she joined the "beat" movement, and later was considered a "hippie." Joplin's alter-native lifestyle led her to the Haight-Asbury section of San Francisco and a recording career which lasted until her death on October 4, 1970, from an overdose of heroin and alcohol.

Joplin's most successful album, *Pearl* (1971) contained her best-known single recordings, including "Me and Bobby McGee" by Kris Kristofferson, and "Mercedes Benz," written by Joplin and Michael McClure.

Joplin returned to Port Arthur for the tenth reunion of her high school graduating class, despite the fact that "they laughed me out of class, out of town, and out of the state, man."

A rock legend and an icon of a generation, Joplin is one of the most influential musicians of all time. Her soulful performances and flamboyant persona continue to engage fans the world over.

Above: Janis Joplin during a press conference at her Thomas Jefferson High School reunion August 15, 1970.

PHOTO BY WATKINS STUDIO, MGC COLLECTION.

Left: Robert Rauschenberg, shown here in 1999, is a world renowned contemporary abstract artist. Twenty one of his works are on view in the Museum of the Gulf Coast's Rauschenberg Gallery.

PHOTOGRAPH COURTESY OF ELLEN PAGE WILSON.

ROBERT RAUSCHENBERG

Robert Rauschenberg's artistic work led a fellow artist to comment, "If this is Modern Art," I quit!" The critic referred to Rauschenberg's "Neo-Dada" style, a combination of painting and sculpture. Others found Rauschenberg's work more to their liking, and paid as much as $7 million for his paintings.

Rauschenberg was born in Port Arthur on October 22, 1925. He studied at the Kansas City Art Institute, the Academia Julian in Paris, and Black Mountain College in North Carolina. He began as an expressionist painter, producing a series of "White Paintings," followed by "Black Paintings" and "Red Paintings" series, which combined brush strokes on canvas with three-dimensional objects attached. These additions ranged from photographs to a goat's head to portions of a bed quilt.

The first living artist to be featured on the cover of TIME magazine, Rauschenberg would become one of the most prolific and innovative American artists of all time. He bridged the gap between abstract expressionism and pop art with his unique methods of painting, print making, sculpture, and performance art. In his later years, Rauschenberg made his home in Captiva, Florida, continuing to create art until his death on May 12, 2008.

L. Q. JONES

Justus Ellis McQueen, born in Beaumont in 1927, adopted the name of L. Q. Jones from the character he played in a film titled *Battle Cry*, based on a novel by Leon Uris.

McQueen was graduated from Port Neches-Groves High School in 1945, then from the University of Texas, where he studied law, business, and journalism. While in college he performed in comedy clubs and roomed with another future actor, Fess Parker.

Parker sent McQueen a copy of Uris' novel when he auditioned for a part in director Raoul Walsh's film version of the story of a squad of U.S. Marines in the Pacific Theatre during World War II. McQueen decided that he wanted to play the part of L. Q. Jones, one of the principal characters in the story usually involved in some humorous activity. He came to Hollywood, won the part, and decided to adopt "L.Q. Jones" as his theatrical name.

After the success of *Battle Cry*, Jones won parts in several films released by Warner Brothers during the 1950s and 1960s, especially in Westerns. He later appeared in such major films as *Ride the High Country* and *The Wild Bunch*, both classics of the Western genre directed by Sam Peckinpah. Jones also played featured roles in such television series as *Cheyenne* and *Cimarron Strip*. He has appeared in more than seventy theatre films, twenty-five television movies, and played scores of single roles in individual episodes of television series.

Jones remains active in film work as an actor, director, and writer based in California, but he is a frequent visitor to his hometown.

Above: Actor L. Q. Jones, a graduate of Port Neches High School, where he was a cheerleader. Jones, whose career spans nearly 50 years, has appeared in 78 motion pictures and dozens of television productions including Hawaii Five-O, Perry Mason, Charlie's Angels, *and* Rawhide. *He has played supporting roles in such classics as* Love Me Tender, Casino, *and* The Mask of Zorro, *creating unforgettable characters along the way.*
COURTESY OF THE MUSEUM OF THE GULF COAST, PORT ARTHUR, TEXAS.

Right: Texaco employees having their annual picnic on Pleasure Island in 1952. Note Port Arthur's silo-like three-hundred-thousand-gallon water tank in upper left hand corner. The U.S. Naval Reserve facility is the barn-like metal building on the left side of the boulevard.
COURTESY OF THE MUSEUM OF THE GULF COAST, PORT ARTHUR, TEXAS.

Above: Port Neches City Hall, 1946, located on the corner of Avenue C and Merriman Street.

Below: Joe Washington, Jr. graduated from Lincoln High School in 1971. He played football for San Diego, Oklahoma, Baltimore, and Washington. Shown are (from left to right): Joe Washington, Jr., his wife Meadowlark, and his father, Joe Washington, Sr.

JOE WASHINGTON, JR.

Joe Washington Jr., remembered as "Little Joe," was an outstanding athlete at Lincoln High School, where his father coached. While in high school, Washington avidly supported Coach Darrell Royal and the University of Texas Longhorns, but enrolled at the University of Oklahoma in 1972 because it was closer to Texas Women's University in Denton, Texas, where his high school sweetheart—and future wife—had enrolled.

Oklahoma's Coach Barry Switzer recognized and utilized Washington's talent from the start. Washington ran for 630 yards during his freshman season, and progressed to 1,321 yards in his senior year. Even as a junior, Washington was named an All-American player by the Associated Press, Football Writers' Association, Sporting News, and other agencies. As a senior, he finished third in Heisman Trophy competition for the best football player in America.

Washington played for the San Diego Chargers, Baltimore Colts, Washington Redskins, and Atlanta Falcons in a career that lasted until his retirement in 1985.

represented by traditional Anglo-Celtic stock, African Americans, Netherlanders, Latinos, and descendants of Old Acadia who came across the Sabine hunting homes and employment in familiar habitats, and later, Asians, fleeing fear—all, from Stilwell's day to Rita's day, seeking, and finding, opportunity on the west side of the Rainbow. Where else would a Brownie have searched?

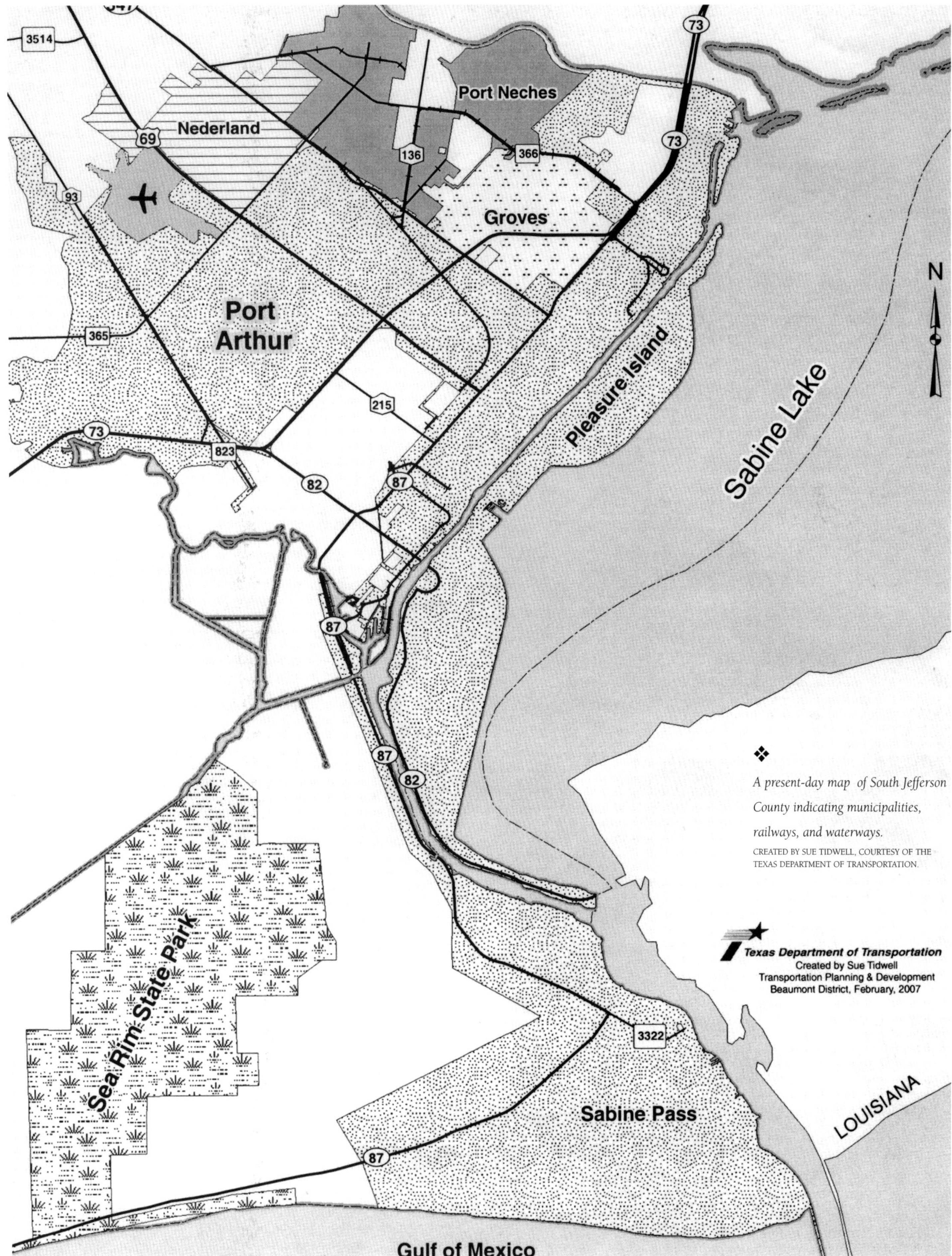

A present-day map of South Jefferson County indicating municipalities, railways, and waterways.

CREATED BY SUE TIDWELL, COURTESY OF THE TEXAS DEPARTMENT OF TRANSPORTATION.

Texas Department of Transportation
Created by Sue Tidwell
Transportation Planning & Development
Beaumont District, February, 2007

Right: A photo of the exterior of the Museum of the Gulf Coast, 700 Procter Street in Port Arthur. The museum is owned and operated by the Port Arthur Historical Society and is dedicated to preserving the Gulf Coast heritage of southeast Texas and southwest Louisiana that links both regions together. The Museum was opened in 1994.

COURTESY OF THE MUSEUM OF THE GULF COAST, PORT ARTHUR, TEXAS.

Below: Mrs. Halvetha Jones, librarian, awarding a certificate to one of the summer readers, Port Arthur Public Library Branch, 740 West Seventh Street, 1957.

COURTESY OF THE MUSEUM OF THE GULF COAST, PORT ARTHUR, TEXAS.

Epilogue

September 2005

Long before the weather service gave them names, tropical storms, especially mighty hurricanes, rearranged the southeast Texas coast dramatically. Arthur Stilwell determined to build an outlet to the world from America's midwest, via his Kansas City, Pittsburgh and Gulf Railroad, but he decided against developing his port directly on the Gulf, electing instead to locate shipping facilities on an inland lake and connect it to the sea by canal. So Port Arthur was founded, and from it came Nederland, Port Neches, Groves, and other communities in the southern portion of Jefferson County.

Hurricanes are accepted by residents of Gulf coastal counties as the price of living where the nearby ocean supplies jobs and recreational opportunities as well as hurricanes; they take the good with the bad, and endured even such mighty blows as Hurricane Audrey in 1957. By 2000, most Gulf Coast residents had learned to store survival supplies—food, water, batteries, etc.—plywood cut to door and window measurements, and to have an evacuation plan awaiting the inevitable need for implementation.

Late in August 2005, Hurricane Katrina flooded New Orleans, virtually destroying the Gulf Coast's legendary playground, and sending hundreds of thousands of south Louisianans scurrying hundreds of miles inland seeking shelter. Residents all around the Gulf of Mexico were on edge; by late September, the season already had spawned seventeen named tropical storms, 10 had become hurricanes of 75 miles per hour or greater, two already had achieved Category 5, the most intense designation on the Saffir-Simpson Hurricane Scale.

In September, three weeks after Katrina came ashore in eastern Louisiana, convection low-level circulation around an upper-level low developed in the Atlantic Ocean east of Cuba. The surface low caused a gradual acceleration of circular winds until September 20, when the disturbance—now and forever remembered as Rita—reached hurricane status. Rita passed over southern-most Florida into

Hurricane Rita came ashore on September 24, 2005, near Sabine Pass, as a Category 3 storm with wind speeds of 120 mph and a storm surge of 10 feet. A group of buildings along Texas 87 in Sabine Pass took a hard hit from the storm's powerful winds, All of Jefferson County sustained heavy damage. Rita had been a Category 5 storm shortly before landfall and was the strongest measured hurricane ever to enter the Gulf of Mexico.

PHOTO BY BRIAN VINCENT,
COURTESY OF THE *PORT ARTHUR NEWS*.

*The Port of Port Arthur warehouse
and dock after 'Rita's' ravages.*
PHOTO BY GUISEPPE BARRANCO,
COURTESY OF THE *PORT ARTHUR NEWS*.

the Gulf, where warm waters gave her energy. She blew west by northwest on a course that angled just northward for a landing between Sabine Pass, Texas, and Johnson's Bayou, Louisiana, essentially the same path taken by her senior sister Audrey nearly forty-eight years earlier. Before reaching land, Rita ratcheted up to 180 mph, the fourth most intense storm on record. Hurricane Hunter Lieutenant Colonel Warren Madden, who flew into Rita's eye through wind gusts up to 235 mph, called her "the strongest storm that I've ever been in." A satellite photo shows Rita filling up the entire Gulf of Mexico from Florida to Brownsville to Yucatan to Havana.

After a century of storms—especially the recent example of Katrina not far away—Texas coasters knew when the time came to evacuate. They boarded up and battened down; loaded what was important, starting with family, pets, and business papers; and started north from Sabine Pass and Port Arthur on Highway 69, blending in those fleeing Port Neches and Nederland. They streamed northward for hours, sometimes as many as twelve hours, before reaching Lufkin or Nacogdoches, only 150 miles away. Motels and hotels were already filled with Katrina's refugees, so Rita's vagabonds stopped at the home of relatives or kept going, some as far north as Oklahoma or Kansas before finding a bed.

Rita came ashore at 2:38 a.m., Central Standard Time, on Saturday, September 24, 2005, with wind gusts reaching 120 mph. She moved up the Sabine River, and then dissipated into a tropical depression that brought heavy rain all the

way to Massachusetts. South Jefferson County lay wet and devastated. Its towns had been evacuated, so few lost their lives directly in the storm. But power was off everywhere, in some places for six weeks. Not a building was left unmarked, and "FEMA Blue" tarpaulins became a familiar and pervasive sight on roofs all over the area. Winds felled more than twenty-five percent of the trees in the area and damaged most of the remainder of them. Fortunately, the storm surge was contained by Port Arthur's levee system on the Texas side of the Sabine; the Louisiana side fared less well. And then came the stillness of storm's aftermath, and heat—98 degrees Fahrenheit. the day after Rita. Without electricity for air conditioning or refrigeration, the area, at least temporally, had returned to its natural setting. South Jefferson County residents found a new way, then, to fix events in time: since September 2005, everything is "before Rita" or "after Rita." Who knows where the Brownies may lead "after Rita?"

POSTSCRIPT
By Shannon Harris, Museum Director

At the time of this printing, Jefferson County, along with neighboring communities along the Texas and Louisiana coast, are recovering from yet another "monster storm." Hurricane Ike made landfall in Galveston, Texas on September 13 at 2:10 a.m. as a Category 2 hurricane with winds of 110 mph. At one point the diameter of Ike's tropical storm and hurricane force winds were 550 and 240 miles, making it the most massive Atlantic hurricane recorded. The unusually large wind field caused Category 4 storm surges. Hours before the eye of the storm reached land, surges of more than 14 feet pounded the coastline. The levee in Port Arthur held once again, saving the City and mid-county residents, but vulnerable communities like Sabine Pass and LaBelle were not so fortunate.

Through various community wide efforts, residents are rallying to aid these devastated areas as well as our neighbors in Bridge City and Orange. Mid and south Jefferson County has seen its share of storms both literal and otherwise, and yet the people of this community continue to rebuild and recover with a resolve and endurance that would make Arthur Stilwell and his pioneering peers proud.

SHARING THE HERITAGE

historic profiles of businesses,

organizations, and families that have

contributed to the development

and economic base of Jefferson County

SPECIAL THANKS TO

Hayes Real Estate

Huntsman

CITY OF
PORT ARTHUR

❖

Right: This aerial view of downtown Port Arthur taken in the late 1930s, shows the rear side of the Municipal Building, bottom center, the city water tower (at left), the Goodhue Hotel (center left), the Sabine Hotel (center right), and the Jefferson County Sub-courthouse (far right).

Bottom, left: The Mary Gates Hospital at 325 Lakeshore Drive was donated in his mother's name by John W. "Bet-a-million" Gates, one of the more influential early Port Arthurians. Built in 1909 and demolished in 1971, the structure served as the Port Arthur Municipal Building from 1930 to 1970, when the new City Hall opened in the 400 block of Fourth Street.

Bottom, right: The Newport Bar on Austin Avenue between Fourth and Procter Streets, was one of the many "Gentleman's Resorts" during Port Arthur's wide-open days of anything goes as long as those in power received their share of the "shakedown." In January 1961, thirty-one-year-old State Reresentative Tom James, of Dallas, shook up Port Arthur and Beaumont when he brought his Commission to town to investigate the open gambling, prostitution and illegal liquor sales that had made the two port cities so popular for visiting merchant mariners.

PHOTOS COURTESY OF THE PORT ARTHUR PUBLIC LIBRARY.

Railroads and safe harbors were the real life stuff that the dreams of Port Arthur were made on. Port Arthur's birth found purpose in the rapid commercial and transportation expansion at the end of the nineteenth century, while its continued growth was fed by the booming oil business of the twentieth century.

Arthur Edward Stilwell already was a legendary pioneer in the fields of insurance, transportation and finance when he came to Jefferson County in 1895. A believer in powers of the psyche, Stilwell's own writings tell how "brownies" came to him in a dream and advised him against purchasing the Houston East and West Railroad. Instead, the pixies told him to build his railroad "directly south from Shreveport."

"Locate your terminal," the spirits told the thirty-six-year-old man, "on the north shore of Sabine Lake," according to information this writer gathered and wrote for the *Port Arthur News* "City Centennial Extra Edition" published on May 28, 1998. "… And there occurred to me a picture of a city…on the north bank of Lake Sabine…here in this landlocked harbor, safe from the most devastating storms, we would create a port," Stilwell wrote.

And so began the history of Port Arthur, named for the man many say was a visionary who "boomed dozens" of towns along the railroad line from Kansas City to the Gulf Coast, said Michael Cate of Looking Glass Media, publisher of *The Centennial History of Port Arthur*, which was released before Christmas 1997.

"His dream, right from the very start, was to get grain, cattle, lumber and goods in and out of the Midwest," said Cate, a native of Mena, Arkansas, which was named for the wife of Stilwell's friend and business associate Jan de Goeijen, a Dutch name that has been anglicized into DeQueen. Today an avenue and an elementary school in Port Arthur are named for her.

Before the railroad was built, weeks of overland travel were necessary for products from the Midwest to arrive on the Southeast Texas Gulf Coast. In many cases, grain and other perishables rotted from being exposed to elements along the arduous journey. Stilwell's dream, Cate said, "was to get it down there in two or three days."

Whether stone or lumber, fertile ground or water, Stilwell used the resources available to create towns and resorts along his railroad. He even solicited editors, offering to finance newspapers in new towns along the route in return for assistance in promoting the new settlements.

The birth of the *Port Arthur News*, the city's last remaining daily newspaper, came as a result of a Stilwell invitation. *The News* actually predates the city by a year; its first edition was printed in a railroad car en route to Port Arthur in March 1897.

When Stilwell began his million-dollar advertising campaign to interest people to come to his "Magic City," invitations were sent to

businessmen throughout the country, urging them to take advantage of opportunities in the new city.

Newspaper advertisements enticed the excursion parties to come to Port Arthur from the Midwest. They came by the hundreds in response to a glowing promise: "A healthy climate, good schools and churches, good farming lands and good markets in which to sell products of the soil are just a few inducements Port Arthur and Jefferson County offer to home seekers."

While the KCS rail line did not open up vast reaches of new territory in the west, it did serve to develop the U.S. frontier by establishing numerous new towns along the tracks connecting Kansas City to the Gulf of Mexico.

KCS acquired more than forty thousand acres on the northern shore of Sabine Lake and the town of Port Arthur was laid out. For paying as much as seven dollars an acre, people laughed at him, local historians say, because the land was nothing but marshes, alligators and hordes of swarming mosquitoes.

The town of Nederland was also founded as a mark of gratitude to Dutch investors. The Mid-County city's name is the German and Dutch spelling and pronunciation for netherland, the descriptive name meaning "low land" for Holland and the five other provinces that together form the Republic of The Netherlands.

Stilwell used four thousand acres for the original plat of the city, which extended from Houston Avenue east to what is now Woodworth Boulevard and from Lakeshore Drive north to Nineteenth Street. The last spike of Stilwell's railroad was driven with great celebration on September 11, 1897. The new city was a mere nine miles from deep saltwater and oceangoing vessels.

Robert Gillham, Stilwell's chief engineer, platted the new town's streets and other improvements. He also was involved in digging of the Port Arthur Ship Canal, which connected

the sea with Stilwell's rails. The canal was completed in 1897 and Port Arthur loaded ships to the extent of 87,632 tons.

In his lifetime, Stilwell founded more than 40 cities and towns, built more than 2,000 miles of new, main-line rails and increased the wealth of the Southwest at the turn of the century by more than $1 billion.

Where Stilwell left off, John W. "Bet-a-million" Gates began.

Gates' interest in Port Arthur started in 1899, when Stilwell needed capital to carry out his plans for the ship canal. From that point on, Gates was involved in nearly every project in the city, including the successful fight of getting Congress to recognize the city as a port of entry. He also had his hand in turning the tiny Texas company into the corporate giant Texaco.

Historical accounts say that Gates and Stilwell were good friends until the gambler outsmarted the city's founder and got Stilwell's part of the railroad. Stilwell left the city and never returned.

After the Spindletop oil well, located between Port Arthur and Beaumont, blew in on January 10, 1901, Gates formed the Texas Company, in which he owned forty-six percent of the stock. Gates urged construction of pipelines and a refinery and furnished $500,000 for the purpose. In addition to forming the Texas Company, he constructed new docks; built the First National Bank in Port Arthur; the Port Arthur Light, Power, and Ice Company; and the Plaza Hotel. He also contributed $60,000 to build Port Arthur Business College, which today is Lamar State College–Port Arthur.

Some say Port Arthur bloomed, while others say it boomed. But during the first half of the twentieth century, Port Arthur grew into a major international port city that welcomed sailors from everywhere and provided them with the "worldly" bounty that seafarers desired when they dock on dry land.

With busy ports in Beaumont and Port Arthur, both cities were "wide open," as local and county elected officials and law enforcement agencies turned their backs to open gambling, prostitution and illegal liquor sales. They were not blind, however, to the envelopes of cash that found a way into their pockets and bank accounts.

While organized crime syndicates from the Northeast came to control New Orleans and Galveston, Jefferson County corruption remained a "home grown" endeavor, repelling any efforts of outside encroachment on the locally owned and operated parlors of pleasure and vice.

The "live and let live" attitude in the town came to a halt, however, when the State House of Representatives General Investigative Committee came to the county in January 1960 to clean up "good 'ol boy" organized lawlessness in Port Arthur and Beaumont.

The investigation was tagged the James Commission because it was spearheaded by thirty-one-year-old State Representative Tom James from Dallas. The nearby Gulf Coast city of Galveston had been cleaned up the year before. The commission's hearings were broadcast live by radio and television, with almost every ear and eye glued to sets that offered more entertainment than any dozen soap operas.

Above: The back, or business side, of the Kansas City Southern Railway Station fills the foreground of this aerial photograph that includes Procter Street and downtown Port Arthur.

Bottom, left: This view of Procter Street, taken in the early 1960s from Beaumont Avenue looking west, shows the city's center of commerce at about the time the James Commission ended Port Arthur's long run as a "wide open" seaport city.

Bottom, right: The Union Saloon, 212 Procter Street, shown during 1906, was another of the local businesses that entertained visiting seafarers and off-work employees of the growing oil refinery industry.

In the end, the gambling parlors and cathouses closed down and bars and nightclubs were forced to obey state laws against the sale of liquor-by-the-drink. Many Port Arthur residents who lived during that era still claim that the city lost much of its allure and grandeur when James left town.

The latter half of the twentieth century was not kind to Port Arthur: a successive string of oil busts knocked the petrochemical industry from its once lofty position, forcing the plants to tighten their belts, computerize processes, and lay off workers by the thousands.

The city also suffered growing pains similar to those challenging other cities in the nation. As the center of commerce shifted away from downtown to undeveloped areas in the outskirts, the white population moved to larger homes and to suburban towns surrounding Port Arthur. As social pressures changed, the African-American community moved into the older neighborhoods vacated by the whites. But with fewer jobs that required more education and training, fewer city residents were filling the precious few industry jobs.

Port Arthur continued to lose retail businesses that moved nearer the higher-paid population in the suburbs. But with the beginning of the new millennium, retail businesses began to return to Port Arthur, along with jobs, although they were primarily for a lower-paid, unskilled local job market.

Several plants announced major expansions in the latter 1990s, which pumped billions of dollars into the local economy and prompted more commercial expansion, including new retail, residential and hotel development, along with oil industry support and subcontracting businesses.

With things looking up, the summer of 2005 brought old realities into perspective. While the city of Port Arthur, nonprofit charity providers and others struggled to provide disaster recovery for Hurricane Katrina victims from New Orleans, a new Gulf hurricane forced those efforts to be redirected as Rita bore down on Southeast Texas and Southwest Louisiana.

After reaching Category 5 strength in the open Gulf waters, Hurricane Rita dipped to the third lowest pressure (897mb) ever recorded in the Atlantic basin. With a flooded New Orleans fresh in our minds and another "storm of the century" looming offshore, Gulf Coast residents from Houston to the Atchafalaya Basin were ordered to evacuate on the morning of September 22. The evacuation routes turned to parking lots and emergency shelters as far north as Texarkana, Fort Worth and Dallas were filled to capacity, as were the hotels and motels.

Most urgent was the evacuation of residents with medical special needs from private homes, nursing homes, assisted care facilities and hospitals. Port Arthur firefighters and police officers went without sleep for days as they cared for those who could not care for themselves. Evacuation ambulances were rerouted to other areas of the state, so quick-thinking first responders called in U.S. Air Force C-5s and C-130s that lumbered, overloaded, from the Southeast Texas Regional Airport until a mere four hours before Rita struck land near Sabine Pass.

About ninety-eight percent of the city's residents were evacuated and were not allowed to return home for almost two weeks, while city crews removed debris and electrical workers struggled to return power to the tens of thousands of customers in the dark.

Damage from Rita is estimated to exceed $16 billion over all, with Port Arthur receiving at least a quarter of that. Intrepid city residents bent into the task of digging and cutting their way out from under devastation that many had never encountered before.

Above: In celebration of the nation's bicentennial in 1976, student artists designed and painted numerous murals on downtown Port Arthur buildings, each with images representative of freedom or the cultural heritage of the city's diverse citizenry. Many of these murals appeared in German director Wim Wender's 1984 film Paris, Texas, *written by Sam Shepard and starring Harry Dean Stanton, Nastassja Kinski and Dean Stockwell.*

Below: Mardi Gras of Southeast Texas attracts more than one hundred thousand visitors to downtown Port Arthur during the annual four-day celebration. This scene of Procter Street taken from Beaumont Avenue in 2002 shows the opening night Mardi Gras crowd for the tenth annual event.

LAW OFFICES OF GILBERT T. ADAMS, P.C.

The Law Offices of Gilbert T. Adams, P.C., is a third-generation professional association of trial lawyers whose concerns and reputations are distinguished by excellence and compassion. The firm recognizes that its clients seek representation after they have been intentionally or negligently wronged.

Sometimes the wrong is an unethical or fraudulent commercial activity by which an individual or corporation has taken unfair advantage of their client. Typically, the wrong is a serious or catastrophic personal injury or death with enormous personal and financial loss. The Law Offices of Gilbert T. Adams provides experience with an unwavering sense of right and wrong, fortified with superior legal experience, enabling justice to be brought against any company or person in the world. The Law Offices of Gilbert T. Adams, P.C., stands committed to just resolutions so that its clients receive the maximum result to which they are legally entitled. These seven attorneys are sought-after speakers, authors, and teachers of trial advocacy and bar leaders. But most important to each attorney is the honorable and successful representation of those who have entrusted their right to the firm's care.

The firm traces its roots to 1930, when Gilbert T. Adams, Sr., returned to his hometown to establish his law practice in Beaumont. Adams was a trial lawyer and prominent legal figure throughout Texas for more than fifty years.

He also was an international leader in securing and preserving human rights. He inspired and mentored many young lawyers, a number of whom joined him in the practice of law. Until his death in 1984, he was a state and national leader of the Bar by virtue of his trial and appellate advocacy, his vital leadership of the Jefferson County Bar Association, the Texas Bar, the Texas Trial Lawyers Association, the International Academy of Trial Lawyers, the Supreme Court Advisory Committee, and his work as a founder of the Association of Trial

Left: This picture was taken around 1940 in the Jefferson County Courthouse. Gilbert T. Adams, Sr., is cross-examining a witness during a trial. while representing a widow, who is dressed in black, in a cause of action concerning the death of her husband.

Below: Denis McCarthy, the comic and creator of the newspaper strip "Little Man" created this sketch. It's humorous depiction Gilbert T. Adams, Sr.'s, humble beginnings as the son of Joseph Dark Adams, a Beaumont wildcatter, and Laure Blanche D'Estaing Devilleneuve.

Lawyers of America, the world's largest association of trial lawyers.

Upon graduating and receiving his Juris Doctor degree and his bar license in 1968, Adams, Jr., returned to Beaumont to join his father's thriving practice. Since that time Adams, Jr., has litigated numerous personal injury and commercial tort cases with multimillion dollar verdicts and settlements, thus causing him to be recognized by his peers as president of the Texas Trial Lawyers Association, president of the Southeast Texas Trial Lawyers Association, member of the board of governors and executive committee of the American Association of Justice, member of the Supreme Court Advisory Committee, Advocate, American Board of Trial Advocates, and many other professional and community activities.

Gilbert T. Adams, III, earned his bachelor of arts degree from Baylor University in 1992 and a juris doctor degree in 1994 from Baylor University School of Law. Upon receiving his law license, he returned to Beaumont to join the firm. He quickly distinguished himself in litigating numerous substantial personal injury and commercial cases with multimillion dollar results, thus causing him to be recognized by his peers in the Million-Dollar Advocates Forum, president of

the Southeast Texas Trial Lawyers Association, member of the board of directors of the Texas Trial Lawyer Associates and frequent lecturer of trial advocacy across the nation.

Catherine Adams Matthews is the newest member of the Adams legacy to join the firm. She is the fourth of Gilbert Adams, Jr., and his wife Marilyn's five children and the fourth of their children to become an attorney. Matthews earned her bachelor of arts degree from Baylor University in 2001 and her juris doctorate from South Texas Law School in 2004. Since 2005, she has been an active member in the firm and the community. She serves on the board of directors to the Jefferson County Young Lawyers and is a member of the Junior League of Beaumont, American Association for Justice, and Southeast Texas Trial Lawyers Association. She is a licensed mediator in Texas, is on the Jefferson County Pro Bono Honor Roll and was licensed in the United States District Court, Eastern District of Texas in 2007.

Each personal injury and wrongful death case that the firm accepts involves extensive and detailed research. The firm's reputation for excellence and compassion is the result of dedicated accomplishments on behalf of its clients for more than seventy years.

The Harlee Williams case, now famous in the annals of Texas jurisprudence, is typical of cases successfully represented by the firm. When Williams' wife, Tullah contacted him to represent her husband in this challenging and deserving case, Adams Jr. was a young lawyer who had practiced only a few years.

Harlee had been notified that his worker compensation benefits were nearing the end of the statutory period of 401 weeks at $49 per week, and Tullah was concerned at what their family of eleven would do when they ended.

"Harlee's scarred forehead overlay obviously displaced skull fragments," Adams remembers. "I learned about the devastating effect of his frontal lobe injury, the occasional epileptic seizures. After years as a responsible and productive husband and father, he was now totally unable to work and too incompetent to care for himself. His wife and children were constantly concerned about his whereabouts, as well as how to manage and care for him. The family was trying to eke out an existence."

Adams began investigating the case—what happened, how it happened, and whether or not it was a preventable injury. He questioned Tullah and tried to question Harlee, gradually realizing what had happened.

"Harlee had stopped his Chevrolet two-ton truck at a rural gas station. While his helper, Kirby Hadnot, was filling the tank, Harlee walked around to check the tires, noticing that the outside tire on the rear dual drive axle appeared to need air. He started to add air to the tire when

the wheels were the ones original to the truck. He found that several manufacturers, including Firestone, Kelsey Hayes, and Bud, made the "RH5" wheels. Because of the time crunch, he had no alternative other than to sue General Motors, Firestone, Kelsey Hayes, and Bud, who immediately hired some of the state's biggest and best law firms to defend themselves.

"It is a rare case, indeed, in which a plaintiff contends that a product was defective but is unable to produce the defective product for inspection and analysis to determine the manufacturer, whether it was built to specifications, and whether it was misused in the market place," Adams says.

Despite this inherent difficulty and the "David and Goliath" aspects of the parties involved, Adams was able to represent the Harlee family successfully and obtain the damages to which the plaintiff was justly entitled as compensation for the injury he suffered.

The Law Offices of Gilbert T. Adams is located at 1855 Calder Avenue at Third Street in Beaumont and on the Internet at www.gta-law.com.

there was a sudden explosion. By the time Kirby reached him, Harlee was lying on the ground, his head bleeding and his body shaking uncontrollably. Kirby thought Harlee was dying.

"The station attendant called an ambulance, and Harlee's life was saved, but his future and that of his family became a nightmare," Adams says. "I was faced with a serious dilemma. I had only a few weeks before the statute of limitations would forever bar the Williams family from filing a products liability lawsuit against the seller and manufacturer of the unreasonably dangerous two-piece truck wheel. The vehicle was a 1962 model manufactured by General Motors, and both it and the wheel that had exploded had been scrapped. Eventually, I was able to get Kirby to locate a wheel 'exactly like' the one that had exploded."

Intensive research revealed that the industry had designated the two-piece truck wheel as "RH5." And it had been nicknamed "The Widow Maker" for its propensity to suddenly and unexpectedly separate during tire inflation or while driving, Adams says. This research revealed that numerous people had been injured or killed by these hazardous wheels.

Although General Motors had manufactured the vehicle, Adams did not know whether

Left: Gilbert T. Adams, Jr., in action.

Below: Gilbert T. Adams, Jr., in front of the Jefferson County Courthouse.

F. B. Taylor Insurance & Real Estate Agency

Above: F. B. Taylor.

Below: Judy Pickett and F. B. and Martha Taylor.

"If it is insurance, we do it!" This is the brief—and very descriptive—motto of F. B. Taylor Insurance & Real Estate Agency.

"It is our purpose to offer the most competitive insurance products available to our customers," says George Taylor. "We want to deliver those products in a professional, friendly, and prompt manner. We feel our staff is the best trained and most knowledgeable of any in the market, and we offer a full range of products, including, but not limited to, personal lines, commercial lines, life, health, and group insurance."

According to Taylor, F. B. Taylor Insurance & Real Estate Agency Inc., the parent corporation,

has three separate locations operating under three names:

- F. B. Taylor Insurance & Real Estate Agency, Inc., 1509 South Highway 69, Nederland, Texas, under the corporate name;
- Carroll R. Hand Insurance & Real Estate Agency, Inc., 411 Miller Street, Anahuac, Texas, and
- Craig Insurance Agency, 1020 Bay Area Blvd., Suite 100, Houston, Texas.

The agency's operation is broken down into four departments:

- Commercial lines: Writes all lines of commercial insurance, including commercial property, commercial general liability, workers compensation, commercial automobile, commercial umbrella, wet marine, and bonds.
- Personal lines: Writes dwellings, homeowners, personal automobiles, recreational watercraft, all forms of recreational vehicles (motor homes, four-wheelers, dirt bikes), antique cars, personal umbrellas, and personal aircraft.
- Life, health, and group medical: Writes personal and business life products, individual medical and dental, long term care, employer-sponsored group health insurance.
- Real estate: Handles primarily residential real estate, although it can also do

commercial properties, and property management. At this time, it handles quite a number of condominiums at Pleasure Island, which are managed as corporate rentals for industrial customers.

When Frank B. Taylor, Jr., who was known by his friends as F. B., returned to his hometown of Port Arthur, Texas, after World War II, he began attending Lamar College in Beaumont. During this time, he met his future wife, Martha Crouch, daughter of Freeman B. and Olie Crouch of Port Arthur. Martha transferred to North Texas State University in Denton, and F. B. attended the University of Texas at Austin.

On December 20, 1947, not long after she received her B.S. degree from North Texas, Martha and F. B. were married at the Methodist Temple in Port Arthur. They lived in Austin until he received his Bachelor of Business Administration degree, at which time they moved back to Port Arthur.

F. B.'s first job was as a ticket agent with Kansas City Southern Railroad, located at the end of Proctor Street and Houston Avenue. Martha worked as a substitute math teacher in the Port Arthur school system. F. B. then sold Chevrolet vehicles at Inman Chevrolet on Proctor Street. Spurred by his love of selling and the desire to own his own

business, F. B. did not have the capital to buy a new car dealership. He had experienced the country's Depression years, so he wanted to sell something the public needed to buy year after year, even when the economy was bad. He considered the grocery business, but again, did not have the capital for this.

In 1955, he formed the F. B. Taylor Insurance Agency "from scratch," in the dining room of his home on Bryan Avenue in Groves. He began as a "captive agent" for Hardware Mutual Insurance Company, but due to some contract changes with the insurance company, decided it was time to strike out on his own.

Above: Sharon Graffagnino, Bill Taylor, Lillian Prince, Jules Goldberg, F. B. Taylor, George Taylor, Vickie Rabalais, and Oralia Cortez.

Below: An early photo of the staff of F. B. Taylor Insurance.

At first F. B. operated the office as a sole proprietorship, and eventually hired one secretary. When George Taylor, F. B.'s oldest son, decided during his sophomore year in college that he wanted to join his dad in the business, he changed his major from engineering to business. He transferred from Lamar University to the University of Texas at Austin, where he obtained his BBA degree in the field of insurance. Upon graduation George sold life insurance with the Aetna Life Insurance Company for a year before joining F. B. in the agency in 1972.

Bill Taylor, the younger of F. B.'s two sons, received his accounting degree at the University of Texas at Austin. While a student he worked part time for the Texas Department of Insurance, but upon graduation became a full-time employee and conducted financial audits of insurance companies for the department. Bill returned to Port Arthur in 1980 to join his father and brother in the agency. The plans were for Bill to assist in opening a surplus lines agency, but something happened.

Bill Craig, a long-time friend of F. B.'s, had been joined by his son, Wally, in Craig Insurance Agency. When Wally was killed in an automobile accident, Bill was sent to Houston to assist in operating the Craig Insurance Agency. He remained in Houston, and after the F. B. Taylor Insurance Agency became incorporated, it purchased the Craig Insurance Agency in 1981, and the surplus lines agency was never formed.

Today, George Taylor, CIC, manages the F. B. Taylor Insurance Agency in Port Arthur, which has fourteen employees, and Bill Taylor, CIC, CPA, manages the Craig Insurance Agency in Houston, which has five employees. Both agencies focus on property and casualty insurance, both personal and commercial lines. The Port Arthur office also handles life, health and group insurance, and sells real estate as well.

F. B. semi-retired in 1978 and was involved in the agency only as a consultant, no longer managing the agency or selling insurance. He died in December 1994.

The Carroll R. Hand Insurance Agency in Anahuac, Texas, was acquired by the F. B. Taylor Insurance & Real Estate Agency, Inc. on July 1, 1997. Dana Finn manages this old-line agency, which was formed in 1947. It offers property and casualty, and life and health products, as well as selling real estate.

The current staff of
F. B. Taylor Insurance.

The Museum of the Gulf Coast tells the extraordinary history of the upper Gulf Coast region with an amazing array of exhibits and programs. Mixing history with popular culture, it offers a memorable experience for all ages. Owned and administered by the Port Arthur Historical Society, the Museum's mission is to collect, preserve, display, and interpret the heritage of the Gulf Coast region between Houston, Texas, and New Orleans, Louisiana.

Although it began in 1964 as the Port Arthur Museum, the Museum of the Gulf Coast opened at its present location with an enlarged scope of exhibits on July 2, 1994. Since then it has continued to grow in visitation, outreach, education and public programming. For more than a decade it has successfully provided an entertaining and educational experience for local residents and tourists alike, while also preserving the rich heritage of a diverse region. Staffed by a small team of full and part-time employees as well as a multitude of dedicated volunteers, the Museum is sustained by a partnership between the Port Arthur Historical Society, Lamar State College-Port Arthur and the City of Port Arthur.

Located at 700 Procter Street in downtown Port Arthur, the Museum's thirty-nine-thousand-square-foot facility contains permanent and temporary exhibits that interpret pre-Columbian to contemporary history, natural history, popular culture and fine and decorative arts. Highlights include a 125-foot mural depicting the Gulf Coast from prehistory to the discovery of oil at Spindletop, prehistoric fossils, Civil War cannons, a pioneer cabin, seashells from around the world, fine glassware, works of art by renowned artist Robert Rauschenberg and the original Fresnel lens from the Sabine Bank Lighthouse. Galleries dedicated to music and sports feature such notables as Janis Joplin and Jimmy Johnson.

The Museum of the Gulf Coast is considered by many to be the number one attraction in Southeast Texas and Southwest Louisiana, linking the two areas together. It is a quality museum like none you have ever seen!

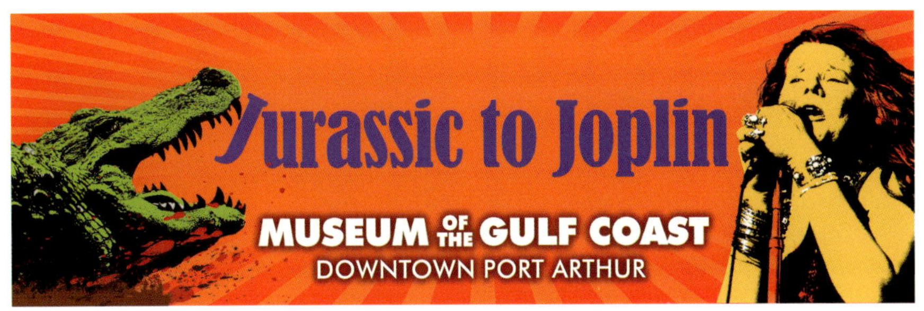

MCM Elegante Hotel and ICA

Starting in 1969 with two used cars on a small lot in Midland, Texas, and branching into the manufactured housing business, John Bushman, with the help of his wife Carol, has weathered the inevitable business cycles of over three decades and continued to grow and expand his business interests in a variety of fields.

John is the founder, CEO, and Chairman of Investment Corporation of America (ICA), which does business as MCM Eleganté Hotel, ICA Homes, ICA Energy, CBS–7, UPN–16, ICA Properties, ICA Realty, MCM Ice, Pace Insurance, Motor City USA, Getaway Spa, MCM Grande, Airline Mobile Home Park, and ICA Wholesale.

The manufactured housing business laid the foundation upon which A-1 and then ICA companies grew and expanded, leading off a winning record of successful businesses that has grown and expanded to include finance, hospitality, insurance, real estate, energy and broadcast.

Key individuals in the early days include:

- Ed Lasater, president of ICA, who joined John in 1975, at the age of twenty-two. Exhibiting the core values of ICA, Ed is an example of the loyalty and respect that John both gives and receives, as evidenced by Ed's climb from a salesperson to the president of ICA.
- John Nichols, who joined ICA in 1982, and is chief financial officer of all the ICA companies.
- Mike Irons, who joined ICA Energy in 1984 and has converted this oil and gas company from a lender against proven reserves into a development company involved in the exploration and recapture of energy properties primarily in Texas, New Mexico, Oklahoma, and Wyoming.
- Barry Marks, who first joined ICA in 1985, has managed a number of the operations listed, and currently operates three television network stations in the Odessa-Midland market.
- Roy Allen, who has overseen management of ICA Properties since 1996 and Music City Mall since 2001. ICA owns approximately sixty percent of all primary business office space in Odessa, Texas, in addition to shopping centers, developed and undeveloped land, and miscellaneous other properties in twenty cities and six states.
- Terry Richards, who has been with ICA since 1995 and has actively managed all office buildings and strip shopping centers in Odessa-Midland metroplex on a day-to-day basis since 2001.
- Donna Simmons, who started with John in the accounting department in 1995 and took the reins at Pace Insurance Agency the following year, selling and issuing policies for manufactured homeowners. Pace currently writes over thirteen hundred policies annually.

- C. D. Smith, who took over as manager of Motor City USA in 2003, after John Bushman reentered the automobile business in 1997.
- Jim Gerard, who has been with ICA since 1996 and manages the manufactured housing operation with wholesale lots in Odessa and Fort Worth.
- Jim Kirk, with ICA since 1984, who operates retail lots in California and Arizona under the name of Homes America.

Individuals who have been key to growth of the company's hotel operations include:

- Marca Washburn, manager of the eight-story, 191-room MCM Eleganté in Odessa since 2000.
- Don Walts, who since 1983 had managed the former Holiday Inn Center in Odessa. He remained as manager when the property was purchased in 2004 and renamed MCM Grande.
- Bill Bianchi, manager of the MCM Eleganté in Beaumont, who assumed that post when ICA acquired the property, the former Beaumont Hilton. During Hurricane Rita, this was home to the area's emergency management operations. Among the many community and charitable activities in which the MCM Eleganté in Beaumont is involved is the Julie Rogers Gift of Life.
- Charlene Swauger, manager of the MCM Eleganté in Albuquerque, New Mexico, formerly the Holiday Inn, since its purchase by ICA in early 2005.
- Michael Burkey, who retained his position as manager of the ICA's most recent purchase, the MCM Eleganté Suites in Abilene, Texas, a property formerly known as the Ambassador Hotel.

The most recent Eleganté purchased by ICA is the former Ambassador Hotel in Abilene, Texas. Michael Burkey remained as manager after the purchase in mid-2005, and is still handling its management.

PORT ARTHUR ABSTRACT AND TITLE COMPANY

For more than a century, Port Arthur Abstract and Title Company has offered both residential and commercial closing, escrow and title insurance services, and is committed to providing customers with a level of satisfaction that is unparalleled in the title insurance industry.

Need for an abstract company to research and maintain records of sales, road grants, mortgages, and other land transactions in Jefferson County was created when Arthur Stillwell platted his namesake, the City of Port Arthur, back in 1895. The Spindletop oil boom at the turn of the century and the real estate development and sales that followed helped to fuel the early success of Port Arthur Abstract.

A. M. Rutan, a local real estate lawyer, who was later joined by a partner, H. F. Banker, founded the company in 1896. After Rutan's death, his son, R. L. Rutan, who was also a real estate lawyer and served in 1942 as Mayor of Port Arthur, succeeded him. Banker's son-in-law, Gil Phares, also an attorney, bought Port Arthur Abstract upon his return from service during World War II. Phares was later joined by his son and law partner, Banker Phares. In 1969, Gil and Banker Phares sold the business to another law partner, Cary Bass.

Following Bass' retirement in 2000, Port Arthur Abstract was sold and has been run by President and Legal Counsel Ken Whitlow and Senior Vice Presidents Molly Mallet, Vicki Robison, and Juliana Stringer. Forty-two employees now serve all of Jefferson County through Port Arthur Abstract and Title Company and Southeast Texas Title Company, which serves Hardin County, as well. These staff members are involved in a variety of civic and charitable organizations and activities, and participate in a wide range of community endeavors.

Originally located at 443 Austin Avenue in downtown Port Arthur, the company moved in 1973 to 3790 Memorial Boulevard and in 1984 to its present location at 2950 Turtle Creek. The decision to rebuild the Port Arthur facility after its destruction by Hurricane Rita in 2005 reflects the company's commitment

❖

Above: Port Arthur Abstract is a historical fixture in Jefferson County.

Below: The company occupied offices at 1790 Memorial Boulevard from 1973 to 1984.

to Port Arthur and Jefferson County. Having invested over one hundred years in the community, Port Arthur Abstract has seen the rise and fall of the local economy reflecting the ever-changing status of the oil industry, which was responsible for the boom that fueled the company's early success. The current boom in the Jefferson County area is the most recent example of this pattern of economic activity. Port Arthur Abstract has risen to the challenge of helping local businesses and industries continue to grow and prosper.

Additional information about the company is available on the Internet at www.portarthurabstract.com, or by phone at 409-727-8871, or fax at 409-727-3954.

Above: The current office, at 2950 Turtle Creek Drive, was rebuilt following Hurricane Rita in 2005.

Below: The firm's current state-of-the-art facility.

The Catholic faith in Southeast Texas began in the mid-1500s, with the arrival of priests who came with the Spanish who came to settle Texas. Father John M. Odin, C.M., came to Texas in 1840 to help establish the Church of Texas. He was the first Bishop of the Galveston Diocese during this era, when Texas had only ten parishes—none of which were in Southeast Texas. From other parts of Texas, priests traveled from one outlying mission to another, arriving first by horseback or buggy, and later, after construction of the railway line, coming by train to minister to Catholics in what is now Port Arthur and other settlements in Southeast Texas.

As early as 1899, the Catholic community in South Jefferson County was served by Father John Gallagher, a priest stationed at Galveston's St. Mary's Cathedral. The first Catholic church in South Jefferson County was dedicated to St. Mary of the Immaculate Conception on September 27, 1903, in Port Arthur. The second Catholic church in South Jefferson County had its beginning delayed due to the 1915 Hurricane. Father Alexis LaPlante, S.S.J., arrived in Port Arthur about the same time as the hurricane in August. High water forced him to move to Beaumont until it was safe to return to Port Arthur and begin Sacred Heart Parish.

By the early 1920s there were a few Catholic churches in Mid- and South Jefferson County. Other parishes grew from outreach of the established churches. Father Fred Hardy arrived

in Port Neches in 1922 as first pastor of St. Elizabeth Parish. Through his hard work, three missions of St. Elizabeth were established in Groves, Port Acres and Nederland. These missions went on to become full parishes.

St. Mary School in Port Arthur was the first Catholic school in South Jefferson County, opening in 1914. Today, Catholic education still has a presence in Port Arthur with St. Catherine of Siena Catholic School, which was founded in 1961. All Catholic schools in the diocese are fully accredited by the Texas Education Association. In 2006 the diocesan schools were honored with a prestigious award from the National Catholic Educational Association.

Healthcare in Port Arthur grew when the Sisters of Charity of the Incarnate Word arrived and took over the Mary Gates Memorial Hospital that became St. Mary, now Christus Hospital–St. Mary. The Diocese also has an active program of social services through Catholic Charities of Southeast Texas that includes the Hospitality Center in Port Arthur.

The current Diocese of Beaumont, which was established in 1966, takes in nine counties in Southeast Texas, including South Jefferson County.

Five bishops have served the Beaumont Diocese—Most Reverend Vincent M. Harris (1966-1971), Most Reverend Warren L. Boudreaux (1971-1977), Most Reverend Bernard J. Ganter (1977-1993), Most Reverend Joseph A. Galante (1994-2000), and

❖

Above: St. Anthony Cathedral Basilica, Beaumont.

Below: Our Lady of Guadalupe Shrine, Port Arthur.

Most Reverend Curtis J. Guillory, S.V.D. (2000-present).

As parishes, missions, schools and health facilities continued to grow so did ministries of the Diocese of Beaumont. Those ministries include education and formation, liturgy and worship, youth and campus, vocations, stewardship, counseling, ministry to the incarcerated and immigration services.

The culturally diversified Diocese of Beaumont now has fifty-two churches representative of many ethnicities, thirteen churches being in Mid- and South Jefferson County. This includes the first Vietnamese parish in the United States—Queen of Vietnam in Port Arthur. Port Arthur is also home to two outdoor shrines dedicated to Our Lady–Queen of Vietnam Shrine and Our Lady of Guadalupe Shrine. Both attract many visitors and travelers each year.

St. Anthony Cathedral Basilica in Beaumont, the mother church for the Diocese, also attracts many pilgrims. In 2004, the Cathedral completed a multimillion dollar renovation and restoration. It was elevated to the status of minor basilica in 2006 just in time for the one hundredth anniversary of the church and the fortieth anniversary of the diocese. In commemoration of those events, Bishop Guillory proclaimed a Year of Jubilee for Catholics of Southeast Texas.

❖

Above: The Shrine to Queen of Vietnam in Peace Park.

Top, left: The St. Anthony Cathedral Basilica.

Bottom, left: Sacred Heart Church at Sacred Heart-St. Mary Parish.

Below: St. Catherine of Siena School.

FivePoint Credit Union

In 1935, fifty people met to realize a dream of building a financial cooperative to provide services to employees of the Texas Company Refinery in Port Arthur. Eight men signed a certificate organizing the Texas Company Port Arthur Works (PAW) Employees Federal Credit union, which opened August 1, 1935.

By 1938, auto loans were offered to members for the first time. The organization affiliated with the Texas Credit Union League (TCUL) and Credit Union National Association (CUNA) in 1940, and obtained insurance covering members' loan payments in case they became disabled or died.

The first office manager was hired in 1956, and in 1960, land for an office was purchased and an office was built at 2349 Memorial Drive, Port Arthur, with additions made in 1975. Continued growth in the credit union followed the implementation of direct deposit and payroll deduction that made it more convenient for members to make deposits and loan payments.

Through the next two decades a variety of economic factors impacted the credit union. Among these was a two-month strike by Texaco employees in 1978 and employee layoffs reflecting the national trend to import oil rather than produce it.

To counter these problems, the TFCU board adopted the Master Charge program; merged

with Texaco Island Employees Federal Credit Union, increasing membership by two thousand, approved adding money to existing loan balances, offered share drafts, money market accounts, and certificates of deposit, reduced loan rates, merged with Port Neches Asphalt Employees Credit Union, offered home mortgage loans, and expanded membership to service and church groups not already served by a credit union. Membership growth in the 1980s led to building facilities at 4401 Highway 73 in Port Arthur.

The 1990s began on a solid financial footing and with continued member service improvements including an audio response phone service giving members twenty-four-hour access to their accounts and an ATM program.

In 1991, Delton Moore retired after thirty-five years as TFCU president, and W. E. (Bill)

Ferrett was named president. His focus was on marketing, member services and increased production. Changes included cash dispensing machines, a new loan origination system, staff training, investment services and insurance. The board approved indirect lending through local car dealerships, first in partnership with CUNA Mutual and Western Diversified, and later independently.

Internal restructuring and staff additions, including a marketing director and an experienced collection manager, improved overall operations. In 1996 the first TFCU branch opened on Dowlen Road in Beaumont. Other changes included a loan phone center, VISA Check Card and in-house intercept process system.

This was the first credit union in its chapter offering eCommerce Home Banking and Bill Payer services, and also provided a security firewall, real-time intrusion detection, and online check imaging.

In 1999, the credit union converted to a community charter and opened membership to all of Jefferson, Hardin and Orange Counties, and led to opening of a Lumberton branch. Service improvements have included a convenient line of credit loan, emphasis on sales in staff training, eStatements, and much more. The community charter was expanded in 2002, adding Jasper and Newton Counties to the membership field. A dedicated mortgage department focuses on in-house first lien mortgages and home equity loans.

In 2003, Erik M. Shaw was promoted to CEO/president, and a senior management team was established with four senior vice presidents, each over a division—lending, operations, accounting/information technology, and human resources. Re-branding of the credit union was discussed for more than a year before its final approval by the board, with the name changing to FivePoint Credit Union. The board of directors also approved two new stores, in Nederland and Bridge City, and began twenty-four-hour loans-by-phone service in a joint venture with CUNA and Appro Systems. The Port Arthur store employees were relocated to improve convenience to members, and additional staff training sessions began.

When Hurricane Rita hit Port Arthur on September 24, 2005, the main office suffered significant damage. Alternate facilities were operational October 5, drive-through lanes opened October 7, and Bridge City and Lumberton stores followed a few days later. A redesigned Port Arthur store was reopened to the public in August 2007 and the grand re-opening of the Port Arthur store was celebrated on September 24, 2007, on the two year anniversary of Hurricane Rita.

FivePoint Credit Union, "America's Financial Convenience Store." For additional information about FivePoint Credit Union, please visit www.5pointcu.org.

The warm breezes of the Gulf of Mexico and Sabine Lake gently ruffle the palm trees on the picturesque campus of Lamar State College-Port Arthur, which includes new modern multimillion dollar buildings, such as the Performing Arts Center and the Carl Parker Multipurpose Center, and unique historic buildings, such as the Ruby Fuller Education Building, built in 1915, and the Gates Memorial Library, built in 1917.

The college was established in 1909 as Port Arthur Business College by John W. Gates, one of the founders of Texaco, to train people for the petrochemical industry, then in its infancy.

The college became Port Arthur Collegiate Institute in 1911, when it was presented to the

Board of Education of the Methodist Episcopal Church North, a forerunner of the present United Methodist Temple.

The church operated the growing campus until 1918, when it was turned over to a nonprofit Texas corporation. This corporation had no capital stock and was overseen by a self-perpetuating board of trustees. The name of the school was changed back to Port Arthur Business College and finally, in 1932, to Port Arthur College.

In 1975 the college joined the Lamar University System as Lamar University Center at Port Arthur. In 1995 the Texas Legislature dissolved the Lamar University System, and Lamar University-Port Arthur along with sister institutions in Orange and Beaumont joined the Texas State University System. In June 1999, the name was changed to Lamar State College-Port Arthur.

Through its nearly one hundred years of existence, the college has provided affordable educational excellence in a hometown setting to thousands of students of all ages, whether they want to complete the first two years of a bachelor's degree program or earn a two-year associate degree or one-year certification to prepare them to enter the workforce.

The college currently offers fifty-seven academic and technical programs, including a diverse selection of career options.

Lamar State students also can participate in a wide variety of student organizations and extracurricular activities including inter-collegiate men's basketball and women's softball.

For additional information on Lamar State College–Port Arthur, visit the college website www.lamarpa.edu.

ECHO MAINTENANCE LLC

Since April 1976, the Roebuck family has been providing industrial construction services, as a general contractor specializing in pipe fabrication and installation, structural steel erection, heavy rigging, and civil work.

Three experienced construction workers, Phillip Roebuck, Jake Miller, and John Morrison, who had worked together for many years for various contractors, invested $15,000 each and utilized their knowledge and expertise to form Golden Triangle Constructors (GTC). GTC was a union company that specialized in municipal and industrial construction.

These men rented a small office in Port Neches. Their first employee was Susie Roebuck, a secretary. Shortly after they opened, they were awarded their first contract, which was a $20,000 municipal project in Port Neches. The company continued to perform municipal contracts until the fall of 1976 when they were awarded a small piping project at Gulf Oil (presently Valero Refinery) in Port Arthur. During GTC's first year, its total sales were slightly over a million dollars.

As the business grew several key people were hired. A few of these people were Paul Roebuck, Richard Dixon, Don Garner, and Lee O. Simms. GTC was now working at Texaco, Union Oil, and Fina Oil & Chemical. Everyone was proud when a new two-thousand-square-foot office was built on Twin City Highway in Port Arthur in 1978.

Phillip bought out his partners in 1981, the same year GTC was awarded its first major projects—revamping two crude units at Gulf Oil and building three units at Independent Refinery in Winnie. Nearly twenty years later GTC would eventually dismantle and re-erect these units at Farmland Refinery in Coffeyville, Kansas.

Above: The installation of a 270,000-pound reactor at Total Petrochemicals DHT Unit.

Below: Echo Maintenance's main office is located at 6711 North Twin City Highway in Port Arthur.

In 1983, Mike Roebuck completed college and began working for the company. He is presently president of Echo Maintenance LLC.

Echo Maintenance LLC was formed in 1987. Echo is a merit shop industrial general contractor. Echo's ten-thousand-square-foot office, warehouses, and equipment yard are located in Port Arthur. Andy Brisendine, who is presently vice president, was one of the first supervisors.

Several sister companies were formed in the 1990s and in 2004. Gulf Coast Fabricators LLC, the company's seventy-thousand-square-foot pipe fabrication facility, is located in Beaumont; Industrial Process Insulation, an insulation and steam tracing company, is located in Port Neches; and Gulf Coast Sheet Metal, a structural steel and sheet metal fabricator, is located in Port Arthur.

Total sales in 2006 for Echo and its affiliated companies exceeded $115 million. The company has averaged 550 employees for the past several years, and is listed in Texas Construction magazines as one of Texas' top hundred contractors. Echo performs projects in Texas, Louisiana, and New Mexico, and the fabrication companies ship products throughout the United States and internationally. Over the past thirty-one years, the Echo family of companies has completed thousands of projects, with total sales exceeding $1 billion.

Noting that his family, especially Susie and Phillip, has given a large portion of their lives building the companies, Mike said Echo has been fortunate to work for most of the area refineries and chemical plants, and to have very dedicated employees.

"We will continue to work safely and service our customer base in the future, and we look forward to passing these companies on to the next generation," he added.

Echo donates to a vast array of local, state, and national organizations, and is very involved in sponsoring youth organizations.

Above: Echo fabricated and erected this ship loader and conveyor system for Martin Las, LLC.

SABINE PASS

Above: A tall ship at Sabine Pass, c. 1897.

Below: The Southern Pacific locomotive Old Mother Hubbard carried freight and passengers to Sabine Pass.

Sabine Pass, Texas, thirty miles southeast of Beaumont in extreme southeastern Jefferson County, was organized by the Sabine City Company and first known as Sabine City. The town site was laid out as early as 1836 and was projected to be a major Gulf seaport.

The first steam sawmill in Jefferson County was built there in 1846, and the Sabine City post office was established by 1847. By the time of the Civil War, Sabine Pass had become a boomtown with major shipments of cattle and cotton. With a newspaper, *The Sabine Pass Times*, and a connection on the Eastern Texas Railroad, the post office adopted the more commonly used name of Sabine Pass and the town was incorporated on June 15, 1861. Sabine, Griffin and Manhassett Forts were constructed during the war to fend off Union attacks there.

An outbreak of yellow fever led most residents to evacuate in 1862, and dissuaded Union troops that had landed near the city and destroyed the sawmill from permanently occupying the area. In the Battle of Sabine Pass, Lieutenant Dick Dowling and forty-six of his men used six cannons to halt another Union invasion in 1863, capturing two Union gunboats, the *Clifton* and the *Sachem*, and 200 prisoners. The gunboats later became Confederate blockade-runners.

By 1880, Sabine Pass was the second largest town in Jefferson County with 460 inhabitants, and its future looked bright when the Sabine and East Texas Railroad was constructed to replace the older rail line abandoned during the Civil War.

Disaster struck in 1886, when a hurricane barreled through the town, killing eighty-six people. Other storms in 1900 and 1915 emphasized the town's exposed position on the Gulf Coast, beginning a decline that continued when the Kountze brothers, major landowners in the area, refused to sell land to prospective developer Arthur E. Stilwell. Construction of the Port Arthur Ship Channel in 1897-98, the subsequent growth of Port Arthur, and the construction of additional deepwater ports at Beaumont and Orange attracted major investors to these rival cities, and Sabine Pass never achieved the prominence its founders had anticipated.

In the wake of the Spindletop oil boom in 1901, the Sun Oil Company built docks and a pumping plant at Sabine Pass, but discontinued these operations in 1927. The Union Sulphur Company, which also built large docks in Sabine Pass, received trainloads of sulfur each day from their mines in Sulphur, Louisiana. Commercial fishing and marine repair remained major local industries.

With the decline of the Spindletop oil field, ships began importing crude oil through Sabine Pass via the Sabine-Neches Waterway to sustain Jefferson County's existing petrochemical industry. Rice, cotton, rubber products, steel,

Left: The towboat Stella in 1898.

Below: The Sun Oil Company loading docks.

Bottom, left: An oil storage tank, filled with petroleum, to be transported to Sabine Pass via pipeline.

Bottom, right: The U.S. Life Saving Station that eventually became the U.S. Coast Guard Station.

sugar, flour, oil, and oil products from the county's inland ports continued to be shipped through Sabine Pass, helping boost the area's economy in the 1960s.

Although annexed by Port Arthur in 1978, Sabine Pass has retained its identity as a community of approximately twelve hundred people. It is home to such businesses as marine service, repair and offshore utilities companies, commercial fishing and shrimping, and also to the fifty-seven acre Sea Rim State Park, which depicts the 1863 Battle of Sabine Pass and offers camping, picnicking and recreational fishing.

Construction has also begun on the Golden Pass LNG receiving terminal near Sabine Pass. Golden Pass LNG is scheduled to be completed in 2009 and will help meet the growing demand for natural gas in Southeast Texas and the nation.

Because of its unique location at the mouth of the Sabine-Neches Waterway and the construction of new LNG terminals nearby, optimistic opportunities await Sabine Pass, its local businesses and residents.

Associated Builders & Contractors of Southeast Texas (ABCSETX) is one of eighty-three ABC chapters nationwide, with its home office in Arlington, Virginia. Nationally, ABC represents approximately 26,000 members; the local ABCSETX Chapter was established in January 1988 and is headquartered at 2700 North Twin City Highway in Nederland, Texas. With 130 members within the industrial sector, ABCSETX promotes pro-business, free enterprise companies by representation in numerous civic and political organizations.

The building that now houses ABCSETX was built in 1959 as a bowling alley called Thunder Bowl and converted in the mid-sixties to the Mecca Club, where the British invasion group The Dave Clark Five and even James Brown played. During its ten-year span as the Lighthouse Club, it offered a DJ booth and a live drummer pounding out the beat. Its mirrored columns, circular dance floor and "traveling wall of lights" made this the Mecca of Southeast Texas dancers and partiers. This complex housed an unusual number of restaurants, bars, and even a beauty parlor. Many area baby boomers are grateful that walls do not talk. During its twenty-plus-year nightclub incarnation, it was also named the Blue Heron and when country/western music took over the area, became Texas Swing before being occupied by ABCSETX.

ABC Training Center.

❖

Left: The newly remodeled front entrance of ABC.

Below: The famous mirrored column on dance floor of "Lighthouse Club."

Today this building is known for offering craft training in welding, pipefitting, electrical, instrumentation, boilermaker, millwright, scaffold builder, industrial insulation and industrial painting. It offers certifications for Construction Site Safety Technician (CSST) and the OSHA 10-Hour, and the Training Center facilitates and administers the nationally recognized NCCER Craft and Pipeline Skills Assessments.

Individuals can work in their chosen craft during the day and earn their craft certification while attending classes at night. All thirty-six petrochemical plants in the Golden Triangle participate in the man-hour contribution program that funds the Training Center.

ABCSETX also participates in many local "school-to-career" programs. Member contractors help sponsor various local high schools by assisting them with training materials and by promoting the construction industry as an alternative to college for young people who opt to pursue a more technical path.

For more information about ABCSETX and its programs, call 409-724-7886 or visit the website, www.abcsetx.org.

ENTERGY TEXAS

In the tradition begun by the Beaumont Ice, Light, and Refrigerating Company in 1888, and continued by Gulf States Utilities, their successor, Entergy Corporation not only supplies electricity but also contributes to the growth and quality of life in Jefferson and twenty-five other Southeast Texas counties.

Just as in the days when horse drawn wagons were the chief mode of transportation and electricity was the new technology promising an end to gas lights, wood stoves and ice boxes in the home, Entergy is committed to providing customers with a safe, reliable supply of electricity.

The company's hardworking crews maintain poles and wires that deliver electricity to its 385,000 customers and those of other electricity providers in the area. Entergy Texas has about twelve hundred employees.

Its employees are actively involved in making their cities and towns great places to live and work. Through Community Connectors, hundreds of employees and retirees in the company's four-state service area volunteer tens of thousands of hours of service annually to improve their communities.

Entergy provides financial support to organizations that address education and literacy, environmental improvement and development, arts and culture and health and social services.

Entergy Texas' impact reaches into other vital areas of the economy, including state and local taxes that provide a major source of revenue for many municipalities.

A major global energy company with power production, distribution operations and related diversified services, Entergy owns, manages or invests in power plants generating over thirty thousand watts of electricity in the U.S. and other countries. Its domestic utility companies deliver electricity to about 2.6 million customers in portions of Arkansas, Louisiana, and Mississippi, as well as Texas.

❖

Above: Edison Plaza Building, headquarters for Entergy Texas.

BASF Corporation has a long history in Texas. The first North American investment by BASF was in Freeport, Texas, in 1958. Today BASF has more than ten sites in Texas. In Jefferson County, you can see BASF's presence at its agricultural products site in Beaumont, and the naphtha steam cracker and indirect alkylation units in Port Arthur. At the Beaumont site, production centers on the agricultural industry with products such as Dicamba, a broad-spectrum, broadleaf herbicide used in maize, cereals and some industrial and non-crop uses.

Further south, BASF collaborates with Total Petrochemicals USA, Inc., and Shell Chemical LP in two joint ventures to produce propylene, ethylene and butadiene. BASF FINA Petrochemicals has one of the world's largest naphtha steam crackers. The plant represents a $1-billion investment by BASF and Total Petrochemicals. The steam cracker produces

propylene and ethylene, often called the building blocks of chemistry.

Next to the steam cracker is the C4 Olefins complex and indirect alkylation unit producing butadiene and alkylate. The complex is a joint venture between BASF, Total Petrochemicals and Shell Chemical. Annually, this facility produces more than 900 million pounds of butadiene and 662 million pounds of a high-octane blending component for gasoline.

BASF and its joint venture partners contribute to the quality of life in Southeast Texas through corporate contributions and volunteer support from employees. Through their many programs and partnerships, BASF is helping to make their community better.

Kansas City Southern

The railroad known today as Kansas City Southern (KCS) was founded in 1887 by Arthur E. Stilwell, a forward-thinking entrepreneur, who went against conventional nineteenth-century wisdom to build a north-south railroad as others looked east-west. His goal was to move agricultural products for export from Kansas City, Missouri, to a port on the Gulf of Mexico and on to European destinations.

Overcoming a host of financial crises, Stilwell's original dream became a reality when in 1897, the Kansas City, Pittsburg and Gulf Railroad Company (KCP&G) was completed. His original plan called for the railroad to terminate at the Port of Galveston, but his vision of a cataclysmic event befalling Galveston led him to rethink his route. What seemed improbable proved prescient as Galveston was largely destroyed by the hurricane of 1900. In the end, KCP&G ran south from Kansas City through Shreveport, Louisiana, and terminated at Port Arthur, Texas, the Gulf port city named for Stilwell.

Later, Stilwell attempted to extend his railroad through Mexico with the goal of reaching the Pacific Ocean port city of Topolabampo. This project failed due to insurmountable construction and financial hurdles. But his dream never died. Today KCS' rail system fulfills Stilwell's dream of reaching Mexico's Pacific Coast. The combination of The Kansas City Southern Railway Company, which operates over 3,200 track miles in the United States and Kansas City Southern de México, S. A. de C.V., which operates over 2,800 miles in

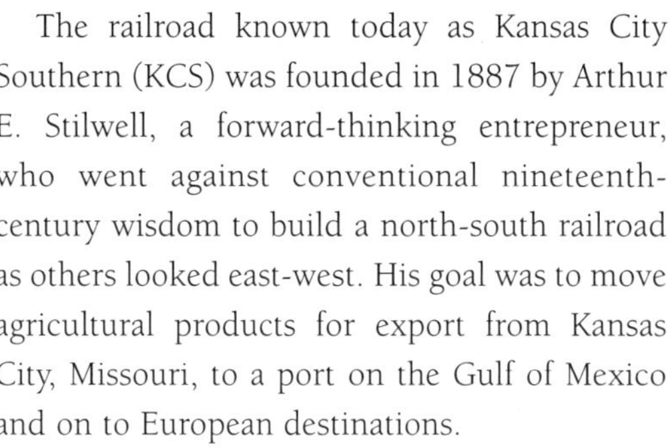

Mexico, forms a railroad network with primary lanes stretching from Kansas City to Mexico City and the port of Lázaro Cárdenas on the Pacific Ocean. KCS also has the most efficient rail corridor between Dallas, Texas, and Meridian, Mississippi, over what is called the Meridian Speedway.

KCS is also a joint venture partner in Panama Canal Railway Company (PCRC), providing transshipment service from the Atlantic to the Pacific oceans on a 47.6-mile railway that runs parallel to the Panama Canal. The world's first transcontinental railroad, PCRC, has been modernized and serves as an important intermodal link for world commerce, complementing the existing transportation infrastructure provided by the Canal. PCRC also operates passenger trains for commuters and cruise ship visitors between Panama City and the Atlantic Ocean port of Colon.

The modern-day KCS has maintained the spirit, vision, tenacity and ingenuity that characterized its founder, Arthur Stilwell. With its unique rail franchise, KCS is rapidly transitioning into a vital component in international transportation logistics. But the one thing that will never change is the company's close identification with the city of Port Arthur.

Above: Kansas City Southern and Big Arthur Crane at Port of Port Arthur.

Below: Kansas City Southern on the Swope Park Bridge in Kansas City, Missouri.

For almost fifty years Earl LaGrappe has been involved in the ownership and operation of Earl's Aluminum in Nederland. The business was started by Earl's father, and Earl began working there on a part-time basis when he was about fifteen years old, gaining knowledge and experience in the business.

After Earl was grown, his father encouraged him to start his own business manufacturing, selling, and installing products ranging from carports and patios to windows and glass rooms. Following those suggestions, Earl set up his own company, but for several years continued helping operate his father's business, which in turn became a father and son business.

"After I got my operation going, I bought my father's business, which primarily involved manufacturing sheet metal," Earl says.

This was about 1987 or 1988, and for a while Earl operated both places, but eventually sold the original site, though he retained the name of Earl's Aluminum, which had become familiar to area residents.

"We're heavily into the sale of storm protection, such as accordion shutters to help protect homes and businesses during hurricanes," Earl said. "We also energize homes to help our customers reduce their electric bills, through the use of energy efficient products, which include windows and glass rooms." Earl's Aluminum manufactures storm windows, window replacement windows, solar screens and window screens.

Earl's Aluminum also does a large amount of metal fabrication for homes, including such things as soffits, fascia, and siding, as well as carports and patios.

"We also manufacture solar and regular window screens, utilizing a state-of-the-art screen machine," Earl says. "We do some sheet metal at this time, and plan to increase that part of the business in the future."

He emphasizes that there is only one Earl's Aluminum. Stop by Earl's Aluminum at 232 Nederland Avenue in Nederland or call 409-724-0461 or 1-800-728-0461.

The Levingstons

❖

Levingston Funeral Home is located at 5601 Thirty-Ninth Street in Groves, Texas. With a second location at 2001 Nall in Port Neches, Texas.

Joel Levingston's roots run deep in South Jefferson County. His grandmother, Louise Lohmann Keeney, moved to Port Arthur in 1904, along with her two brothers, Henry and Ed Lohmann. The brothers established The Home Laundry, and Louise ran the office. The family also purchased land in the Hamshire area, raising cattle and Quarter Horses.

Joel's father's family moved to Port Arthur in 1913. The family produced many mariners and founded Levingston Shipbuilding in Orange. Joel's father, Captain S. W. Levingston, went to sea as a teenager, rose through the ranks, and retired as a Sabine Pilot with the longest tenure of any pilot. Joel's grandfather and uncles were also captains of tankers sailing under the flags of Gulf and Texaco.

Portia moved to Port Arthur in 1936 from Central Texas with her parents, Porter and Annabelle Brock Smith. Her mother's family were Texas pioneers who settled in Lockhart, where their log cabin home remains with a historical marker. The exploits of the Brock and Withers traildrivers are featured in numerous historical books.

In 1955, after returning from service in Korea, Joel realized his childhood dream of opening a funeral home. He and Portia founded Levingston Funeral Home, with the backing of Captain S. W. Levingston, Curtis Moerbe, and O. W. Burton. In 1957 the funeral home was destroyed by a tornado, and the young couple rebuilt at its current location in Groves.

For five decades, Levingston's has been known for their care and compassion. In the 1980s they acquired a second location in Port Neches. Today the firm is one of the most successful funeral establishments in the state. Their two children, Kathy and Jay Levingston, have joined their parents in the operation of the business.

The Levingstons are active in regional, state, and national funeral associations. His peers recognized Joel as "Funeral Director of the Year" in 1997.

The family continues the tradition of raising cattle and Quarter Horses and devotes much of their time to community affairs, helping to make Mid and South Jefferson County a better place in which to live.

The Port Arthur Works was a direct byproduct of the January 10, 1901, Lucas gusher and the resulting Spindletop oil boom in Beaumont, Texas.

The Texas Fuel Company was started by Joseph Cullinan and Arnold Schlaet to sell Spindletop oil with additional investment from John W. ("Bet-a-Million") Gates and others. The company went into business on January 2, 1902. When it was decided to build a refinery, more investment was needed. In March 1902 a new corporation, named The Texas Company, took over the assets of The Texas Fuel Company valued at $1.25 million, and on April 7, 1902, The Texas Company was incorporated with a capitalization of $3 million.

Construction of the new refinery at Port Arthur was started in November 1902. With the dramatic decline in Spindletop production in late 1902, most of the new company's investment capital was risked drilling wells at Sour Lake and was rewarded with a gusher on January 8, 1903. The refinery was completed and started up on November 13, 1903.

The bankrupt Port Neches refinery was purchased by The Texas Company in 1906 and restarted as an asphalt refinery. The Port Arthur Terminal, called "The Island," had a canning plant to produce metal cans for filling with products from the refinery. Ships left the terminal carrying products bound for Europe, Africa, and the Far East.

The Port Arthur Refinery played a major role in producing products for the war effort in World War II, with lube oil being one of the major products. In 1989 a joint venture with Saudi Refining, Inc., was formed which was called Star Enterprise. In 1998, Shell Oil Company was brought into the joint venture under a new name, Motiva Enterprises LLC.

Over the past two decades the refinery has been streamlined and modernized in an effort to make it a world-class refinery. A major focus was on producing lube base oils with new processes and units added. It is now the largest lube base oil producer in the world. A major investment project is being planned that will more than double the size of the refinery, making it the largest refinery in North America. Many construction jobs and additional permanent jobs will be created, which will provide a more stable local job market.

Motiva stands committed to its employees and neighbors to provide quality of life opportunities in our community.

When Morris Weeks began his own welding test lab business and welding school on November 15, 1986, his timing was great for obtaining equipment at a bargain price, but poor for getting work in his field.

"We qualify welders for petrochemical and marine industries," he said. "We write procedures for the proper way to weld and train welders in all processes, including shielded metal arc, gas tungsten arc, and flux cored arc."

Things were so tight in the early days of his company that one Tuesday morning he told his secretary, Theresa Austin, that if the situation did not change by Friday, he was going to shut down.

Austin said she would pray the rosary that night. On Wednesday morning a Houston man called and asked if Weeks could test about two thousand welders. After they sent nine hundred tests a month for two months, he called and told them he could not continue because his equipment was breaking down and had to keep up with material flow. They replied that was fine, for he had just finished testing the last of their group.

This early boost from the American Petro Fina expansion allowed Weeks to get out of debt and continue building his business, which is located at 4405 North Highway 347 in Nederland. His future plans are to build a separate training facility across the street, with testing to remain in the present location.

Along with his two daughters, Wendy Nobles and Angela Atteberry, who helped him get the business started, he lists Austin and D. P. Cordell as key components to its success. When Austin was hired as his secretary, she planned to stay only a couple of years while she finished college so she could teach school. Eleven years later she completed her education, remaining with Weeks. Weeks calls himself the "Grandboss" of Austin's children.

Weeks is active in the community as a Shrine clown, a Confederate soldier in Civil War re-enactments, a Mason, and a Shriner. Weeks took students to Veterans' Memorial Park for four years to build flagpoles, flag stands, work on the Tower of Honor frame, sandblast and paint the cannon. In his spare time he is a beekeeper, and has taught welding at Lamar Institute of Technology for twelve years. He is also on the advisory committee of Angelina Junior College in Lufkin, and the Lamar Institute of Technology in Beaumont, and is involved in numerous area high school welding programs.

A kid-friendly atmosphere is obvious at The Dental Dock in Port Arthur. The office is decorated in bright colors, with a video arcade called "The Dive," television sets on the ceiling over treatment beds, a bright yellow boat called "Tooth Ferry" in the waiting room, a reception desk in the shape of a big red tugboat, and even flooring that looks like a dock and blue water. Of course, the equipment is child-friendly, too, with such things as digital x-rays and an air abrasion unit for "drill-less" dentistry.

George G. Scott, Jr., D.D.S., pediatric dentist, and Roya Wood-Scott, D.D.S., general dentist, conceived the idea for The Dental Dock during the early days of their practice. Then located in a two-thousand-square-foot space in the Mid-Jefferson Hospital professional building, their ocean theme facility had wave-patterned wallpaper and a big boat in which patients could play in the waiting room.

They bought a lot next door to a fire station on Ninth Avenue in Port Arthur, and retained a Beaumont architect to draw up construction plans for a five-thousand-square-foot lighthouse-shaped, free-standing building. Scott designed the décor to carry out that theme, and on June 1, 2005, The Dental Dock was born.

As a pediatric dentist in the Golden Triangle, Scott treats children and adolescents. He also provides hospital-based dentistry for patients with special needs. The Dental Dock's 11 employees serve over 17,000 patients. Since his practice is now at its maximum size, Scott plans to add a second pediatric dentist within the next five years.

Active in community and charitable organizations, The Dental Dock participates in Beaumont's Kidfest, Nederland Health Fair, Mid-County Kinderventure, and in field trips and educational events.

The Dental Dock's mission is to provide the highest quality dental care for children, adolescents, and special-needs patients of any age, in a positive, nurturing environment, to gain the trust of patients and develop a long-lasting relationship.

"We will listen respectfully to your needs and concerns to provide the highest quality, personalized service," he says. "It is our goal to always incorporate fun and comfort while delivering dental treatment."

Above: A bright yellow boat called "Tooth Ferry" awaits the patients of The Dental Dock.

Below: The Dental Dock is located at 7860 Ninth Avenue in Port Arthur.

A direct importer of fine European antique furniture and objects d'art, Snooper's Paradise at 5509 East Parkway, Groves, Texas, also carries top lines of reproductions, including Althorpe, Maitland Smith, Thedore Alexander, Habersham, and fine chandeliers by Schonbek, Savoy and John Richards.

In the early 1950s, John Hampton helped the Service League Charity of Port Arthur by purchasing second-hand furniture and setting up a shop for them on Ninth Avenue. Having developed a love for antique furniture, Hampton opened a store on Bluebonnet Avenue in 1952 purchasing items at estate sales in New Orleans, Philadelphia and Boston to stock his store.

His son, Jon, joined him in the business in 1959 and they made their first buying trip to Europe. Since that time they have purchased almost exclusively in Europe, making several trips annually. Jon's wife, Terry, joined him in business as a vice president in 1975, and they have made buying trips together to Holland, England, Belgium, Italy, France, Germany, Hong Kong, China and India. Jon's son Scott joined the business in 1987.

Snooper's was among the first U.S. importers to use SeaLand Containers for shipments from Europe.

Snooper's primary customer base encompasses Texas and Louisiana, but sales and shipment sites have also included Florida, Washington, D.C., California, and Alaska.

Liberace was among Snooper's famous customers stopping by in 1960, while he was in Port Arthur to present a concert. Casually dressed in blue jeans and a pullover, rather than his trademark glittering attire, he purchased many of the best pieces on display, and had them sent to California.

Many of Snooper's ten staff members have been with the business for over thirty years. Among them are Mary Nell Dore, Jean Duplantis, Pat Sheppard, and Barbara Ryan. More recent additions are Shirley Adams and Byron Broussard.

Thanks in part to their goal of providing the highest quality and selection of antique and new merchandise to clients at the most reasonable prices possible and providing exemplary service, Snooper's has grown from a 5,000-square-foot building and $50,000 in annual sales to a 30,000-square-foot showroom and sales of over seven figures.

In the 1880s, Alex Broussard, owner of A. Broussard Livery Stable, opened the first family funeral parlor in Southeast Texas. As was common, undertaking services evolved naturally from livery establishments, since both businesses required horses and carriages. As Southeast Texas grew, thanks to logging and the discovery of oil at Spindletop, Broussard's first wood-framed parlor was soon replaced by a large brick facility in downtown Beaumont.

In the 1920s, Alex Broussard was succeeded in the family business by his son, Dale. In the fifties, the founder's grandson and namesake, Alex Broussard, and his brother James Broussard joined the firm. By the early 1980s, the family vocation was in its fourth generation when Jim and Tom Broussard joined the company. Blue Broussard, great-great grandson of the founder has now established the fifth generation of Broussard's service to southeast Texas families.

Prestige in their field is evidenced by the firm's membership by invitation in the Selected Independent Funeral Homes organization, which consists of independent funeral directors selected for membership based upon their high standards of excellence. The firm was honored in 2000 for over fifty years of membership and service to the organization. Professional recognitions for the Broussard family and staff include two Governor Appointments and Presidencies of the Texas Funeral Service Commission, Board Members and Officers, including President of Selected Independent Funeral Homes, Texas Funeral Directors Association, and Southeast Texas Funeral Directors Association including two Funeral Director of the Year accolades; and the Federal Emergency Management Agency's Regional Disaster Mortuary Team appreciation for outstanding performance immediately following the Oklahoma City bombing. In 1998, Broussard's was presented the inaugural Torch Award for Marketplace Ethics by the Better Business Bureau of Southeast Texas.

In 1995, Broussard's acquired the former Davis Funeral Home in Nederland. This facility is located in a stately home built in 1912 by the late Judge John McNeil, and has served as a funeral home since 1945. Craig Melancon then joined the Broussards to care for the families of mid and South County, and in addition to his dedication to Nederland, now serves as the firms General Manager. Born and raised in Port Arthur, Craig has received numerous accolades, including "Small Business Person of the Year" by the Nederland Chamber of Commerce, "Funeral Director of the Year" by the Southeast Texas Funeral Directors, and several state committees with the Texas Funeral Directors Association.

The family has truly come full circle, now serving all of Southeast Texas just as Alex Broussard did over a hundred years ago. The company has two facilities in Beaumont and other locations in Kountze, Nederland, Silsbee, and Winnie. Broussard's has recently added its own Crematorium to better serve families who desire cremation, and to give them a nice family atmosphere for a final committal.

Above: Craig Melancon.

Below: James Blue Broussard, III.

Stoneburner-Verret Electric Co., Inc.

For ninety-four years, Stoneburner-Verret Electric Co., Inc., has served residential, commercial, industrial and institutional electric markets with design, installation and repairs. Its complete lighting showroom offers state-of-the-art fixtures and parts, and an electrical supply warehouse stocks hard to find, as well as common electrical items. Stoneburner-Verret, Southeast Texas' premier electrical, data, telecommunications and instrumentation contractor, offers 24-hour emergency service, 365 days a year.

The company was ounded by F. E. "Stoney" Stoneburner at 600 Proctor Street in 1913. Upon his death, his son Frank took over the business. In 1948, Frank sold the business to Joseph A. Verret, Sr., and Joseph A. (Jack) Verret, Jr. Renamed Stoneburner-Verret Electric Co., it was operated as a limited partnership. After Joseph, Sr. passed away, the company was incorporated with Jack as president and Beverly Verret as vice president and secretary-treasurer. Under their leadership, it expanded three times, adding additional warehouse and garage area, a gifts showroom, and a state-of-the-art, full service lighting showroom representing over 154 different lighting companies. Stoneburner-Verret now occupies over 43,750 square feet under roof. A portion of its space is the framing members of the Texaco Island grain silo. Steve Verret, who joined the company in 1973 and was named vice president in 1989, purchased the company in 1991. It currently operates under six generations of continued family ownership.

Stoneburner-Verret is committed to on-time, in-budget performance for all customers, and to forging and maintaining lasting relationships by providing complete and professional service.

"We provide qualified, trained professionals at all levels," Steve says. "Our field technicians are fully trained and licensed. Many are further certified in specialty areas (high voltage splicing, digital programming, motor controls, and data/communications) to serve customers' evolving needs. For many, our technicians are further trained to operate and maintain customer-specific systems, such as software for motor or lighting controllers."

Emphasizing safety for customers and employees, the operations staff fully supports logistic requirements of all projects. Professionals staff the accounting department to provide needed items on a timely basis. Project managers are all master electricians who know how to assemble and coordinate the company's team to ensure unified, well coordinated projects.

Stoneburner-Verret supports the community through a host of activities and organizations.

Reared in Nova Scotia, within sight of the Atlantic Ocean, Captain Roderick D. Steele went to sea at an early age, and worked his way to become a ship captain with a "Master of All Oceans" license. In 1900 he retired to Port Arthur, one of his favorite ports of call, and became involved in the marine insurance business, providing protection for hulls, liability and cargo. The National Cargo Bureau of New York appointed him as its representative for the ports of Sabine, Orange, Beaumont and Port Arthur, to make certain ships were properly loaded to prevent cargo shifts at sea.

In 1924, Captain Steele hired Julian Salter, a young Port Arthur College graduate who had previously worked as a butcher, oilfield roughneck, and Texas Company refinery worker. Salter was a natural in the insurance business. The firm, which also sold real estate, became known as Steele, Salter & Company. Their biggest transaction involved sales of small sections of Interurban right-of-way that had cut through hundreds of back yards and lots in Port Arthur. When the rail was discontinued, the property was sold to adjoining property owners.

In the late 1930s, E. A. Bunge, a Dutch land banker, opened a branch of the Holland-Texas Hypotheek Bank that replaced loans previously provided by Port Arthur Land Company and Port Arthur Town Site Company. Salter and Elizabeth Ballard became bank officers, and Bunge joined the insurance firm, which became Steele, Salter, and Bunge.

The insurance agency grew under Julian Salter's leadership, diversifying into all aspects of insurance, and becoming Julian Salter Company. One of Salter's two sons, Julian "Clayton" Salter, became active in the agency in 1952, and still serves as an advisor to the agency. Slater's other son, Neil T. Salter, chose automobile finance.

The Julian Salter Insurance Agency, located at 3230 Central Mall Drive in Port Arthur is now owned by Clayton's son, Stuart Salter, who has twenty-two years' experience in the industry. It offers all types of insurance and insurance products, as well as risk management and loss control safety programs.

Above: Julian Salter.

Below: Captain Roderick Steele.

AMERICAN VALVE & HYDRANT

American Valve & Hydrant (AVH) has been part of Beaumont, Texas', business community since 1951, when a local businessman purchased a small tract of land and built a foundry at 3350 Hollywood Avenue.

American Cast Iron Pipe Company (ACIPCO) of Birmingham, Alabama, bought the site in 1969, and began an extensive building and modernization program. The thirty-eight-acre site now includes a large, modern shop utilizing CNC equipment, and assembly areas for all its products.

Complementing its production of steel and ductile iron pipe, the Beaumont facility allowed ACIPCO to offer a complete line of waterwork products to its customers. Waterwork valves from 2 inches to 66 inches, fire hydrants, tapping sleeves, indicator posts and a complete stock of parts are built at AVH.

Several truckloads of quality valves and fire hydrants from AVH are shipped each day to customers and distributors throughout the

PHOTOS COURTESY OF THE PORT ARTHUR PUBLIC LIBRARY.

United States and around the world. AVH is the only hydrant manufacturer in Texas. As an affiliate of ACIPCO, it supports one of the world's largest manufacturers of pipe, valve and hydrant products for water, sewer, gas transmission and industrial markets.

In 1997, AVH became registered to the ISO 9001 Quality Standard. Regular audits are conducted to ensure documentation and procedures are current and meet the ISO 9001 standard and requirements.

AVH adds state-of-the-art equipment regularly. Its employees receive continual training, good pay and other benefits.

The unique Christian principles that have guided ACIPCO's operation since 1905 have also influenced the management culture at AVH. The "Golden Rule" philosophy, promoted by ACIPCO founder, John J. Eagan, encourages employee involvement in the community.

A long-time business partner in the School Volunteer Program of the local public schools, AVH encourages people from all levels of the company to serve on boards and committees of organizations such as United Way, March of Dimes, Chamber of Commerce and education initiatives. Employees are always ready to conduct fundraisers to help with special needs that may arise in the community.

American Valve & Hydrant takes pride in its heritage, and in serving the needs of industrial and municipal customers throughout the United States and worldwide.

The year was 1901 and Port Arthur was little more than a fishing community and a small commercial port. But things were about to change…

On January 10, 1901, in a field about fifteen miles to the North, a wildcat driller named Lucas sunk a drill bit into a pool of crude oil that would spew a "geyser" of "black gold" that would take nine days to tame. At the time, the driller was working with money supplied by two business partners, John Galey and James Guffey. These two industrious individuals soon parlayed ownership of their Spindletop oil leases into a deal that would form the Gulf Refining Company of Texas. Soon after, two crude oil stills were built in marsh land located west of Port Arthur and the Port Arthur Refinery was born.

Though ownership of the Port Arthur Refinery has changed throughout the hundred-plus years of its existence, the refinery has seen and participated in the innovation and evolution of the oil refining business. Presently, though no longer the largest refinery in the world, it remains one of the largest and most advanced on the Gulf Coast. As for the future, Valero Energy Corporation, current owner of the facility, plans to continue to develop the facility as part of its long range plans to produce high quality transportation fuels.

Finally, any mention of the Port Arthur Refinery has to note the fact that the success of the operation has involved more that just concrete, iron and crude. Throughout the years, literally tens of thousands of Port Arthur and Southeast Texas residents have worked at the refinery and many present employees can trace their ancestry back to the original builders of the first crude stills. This legacy of loyalty and dedication combined with years of industrial innovation has served to ensure the continued growth of both the Port Arthur Refinery and Southeast Texas.

Valero Energy then and now.

The mission of the Schooner Restaurant, Inc., is simple: To provide our friends and neighbors the freshest seafood and finest steaks in a casual, friendly atmosphere with superior service.

Organized in 1947, this outstanding, family-operated seafood restaurant and steakhouse specializes in serving local Gulf seafood.

The Schooner originally operated with a very limited menu that included gumbo, beer, and a few other items after its opening by Luke LeBlanc.

In 1950, Eugene Megas purchased the restaurant and expanded the menu, a change much appreciated by its customers. In 1959 a fire forced the restaurant to close temporarily but it was rebuilt in 1960. The Schooner is now owned by Constantine S. Megas, who purchased the business in 1968.

Like other businesses in mid-Jefferson County and elsewhere, the Schooner has been subject to a number of economic challenges through the years, but has survived despite strikes that depressed the local economy in the 1960s and '70s and the oil bust in the '80s.

Weather-related damage from Hurricanes Audrey and Rita added other trials, as has the national trend toward competition from corporate chains.

Despite all this, the Schooner continues to grow, now boasting forty-five to fifty employees to serve customers drawn from markets in Houston, Dallas, Austin, and elsewhere.

"In addition to those who have always been our loyal customers, we are now serving their children, grandchildren, and great-grandchildren," according to Steve Megas, the Schooner's vice president. "Our sales were the best in our history during 2006."

Located at 1507 South Highway 69 in Nederland, the Schooner provides southeast Texas with a superior dining experience, and plans to continue doing so for many years to come.

According to Megas, the Schooner Restaurant is a success because of the hard work and dedication of his parents, Constantine and Antonia Megas. "They worked vigorously day in and day out to provide for their family," he said. "They are what the American Dream is about."

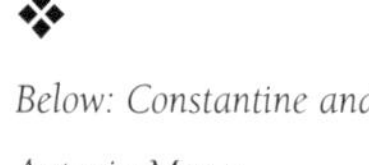

Below: Constantine and Antonia Megas.

Realizing that pre-assembled mats of timbers would work much better than loose lumber, Joe Penland, Sr., first began to put timbers together in his mother's backyard in Nederland to form mats. His first mats were designed to help crane operators gain access over soft soils. The idea quickly caught the attention of customers in every sector of the construction and transportation industries and Quality Mat Company is now the largest producer of mats and one of the oldest companies in the business.

"We've been there since the beginning," says Penland, who formed the company in 1974 to provide temporary road and work surfaces for construction sites.

Based at 6550 Tram Road in Beaumont, Texas, the company annually produces over 150,000 mats, and its products carry exclusive patents that serve a variety of major industries. In 1980, Quality Mat developed the interlocking mat system that is pre-assembled for rapid installation and de-installation, and assembled as two-ply, three-ply or parallel lumber units.

"These products have revolutionized the matting industry and provide key advantages over conventional loose lumber surfaces," Penland says. "First, they provide increased stability and smoothness. The interlocking design distributes weight and transfers shock over a large surface area and keeps the mats from slipping or sinking under heavy loads.

"Second, the mats save our customers money because of the reduced time it takes to lay down and remove them at a job site, their improved durability and longevity over other matting products, and the increased protection they provide to equipment and the environment."

At Quality Mat Company, the mats are made from the best materials, including furniture-grade oak and other hardwoods, stainless steel fasteners or bolts, and are assembled in the company's field-proven, patented configuration.

"Our mats are designed for the most rigorous industrial applications and the most brutal conditions of oilfield exploration and construction sites," Penland says. "When you need to gain access to difficult terrain or protected geography, Quality mats can't be beat. Our mats outlast conventional mats because we start with the best lumber available and build them by hand to maximize and enhance the natural strength of southern oaks."

Sutherlin Jewelers

The nterior of Sutherlin Jewelry at 520 Procter Street in Port Arthur, 1952. Store personnel shown are (from left to right) Mrs. Urcy Harmon, salesclerk; Charles Morgan, watchmaker; Jim Sutherlin, manager; Edgar B. Sutherlin, owner; and Elizabeth Anne Sutherlin, daughter of Jim.

Edgar B. Sutherlin, with his family, moved from Culver, Indiana to Orange, Texas, in 1913, and opened a jewelry store. It was only a few months before Ed noted the booming oil refineries in Jefferson County and the family traveled on the train to Port Arthur in 1914. The first jewelry shop was in Hart Drug store in the Stock Building at the corner of Procter and Austin Avenue. Business prospered and Ed's brother, John, also a watchmaker, came from Indiana and joined him. The popular jewelry store soon relocated to 514-520 Procter Street. In addition to quality watches and jewelry, musical instruments, sheet music, and luggage sales complemented the business.

To perpetuate an old English custom the Sutherlins installed a large town clock with a four-foot diameter face in front of their store. The clock became a landmark and provided continual public service for decades. Edgar and John retired in 1955 to work in their garden and to travel. Edith and Edgar reared three children—Maurine, Waneta, and James.

Milton's Texaco

Milton and Sonja McCreery has seen many changes since October 1, 1965, when they first opened Milton's Texaco Station at 3949 Twin City Highway in Port Arthur. All stations offered full service then, but in the Port Arthur-Port Neches-Groves area only Milton's now provides everything from state inspections and fixing flats to lube, oil, and filling the gas tank.

"Gas prices then were 23.9 cents a gallon for regular and 27.9 cents for super," he says. "During gas wars in the late 1960s, prices dropped to 20 cents. And, in the 1970s fuel shortage, gas lines were half-a-mile long."

Milton now has two self-service islands and one island offering full service at a slightly higher price, "Of course we always pump gas and provide other services for the handicapped," he says.

Many people now "price shop" or "location shop," but many of Milton's customers—including some who have never put gas in their cars—have been with him from the beginning."

Milton's children, Kent and Tammi, and now his grandchildren, Kandice and Lani Appaleman, have been involved in operating the station. Even though the business requires twelve to fourteen hour days, he says, it has been good to him.

The spirit and personality of Percy Villemez infused Percy's Café, even though he would have said they reflected John Wayne's film depictions of American ideals. Percy revered Wayne, displaying photos, figurines, postcards and other memorabilia of the actor, testimony of his implicit belief that "The Duke" stood for America, hard work, fairness, and the possibility of achieving whatever you really wanted.

Percy left the security of a refinery job to start a construction business that eventually led to Percy's Café at 5991 Jade Avenue in Port Acres. Also a convenience store, this was a gathering place where neighbors, refinery shift workers and visitors could enjoy home-cooked plate lunch specials with Texas-size portions twenty-four hours a day, seven days a week.

Vehicles outside ranged from battered trucks to luxury cars, attesting to the variety of customers.

Before his death in December 2006, Percy became a true entrepreneur, owning Percy's True Value Hardware and Feed Store, a car wash, motel, auto parts house, muffler shop and auto repair shop, some land, and rental houses. He joked that with each acquisition there was more room for the Duke.

No longer open due to damage from Hurricane Rita and Percy's very poor health at the time, Percy's Café is now only a memory.

Percy Villemez.

SPONSORS